NURSERY STYLE

Creating Beautiful Rooms for Children

■

Annie Sloan and Felicity Bryan

CONTEMPORARY
BOOKS

CHICAGO · NEW YORK

Throughout this book, we refer to children using masculine pronouns, such as he *and* his. *Please keep in mind that we are referring to your daughters as well as your sons.*

Library of Congress Cataloging-in-Publication Data

Sloan, Annie 1945–
Nursery style, Creating beautiful rooms
for children/Annie Sloan and Felicity Bryan.
p.   cm.
Includes index.
ISBN 0–8092–4282–6
1. Children's rooms.   2. Interior decoration.
I. Bryan, Felicity.   II. Title.
NK2117.C4S5   1989
747.7'7–dc20   89–31864 CIP

Published by Contemporary Books, Inc.
180 North Michigan Avenue, Chicago Illinois 60601
Manufactured in Great Britain

Typeset in Linotron 202 Bembo
by Wyvern Typesetting Limited, Bristol
Printed in Italy by L.E.G.O. Vinenza
Designed by Elizabeth Ayer

for Henry, Tom, Alice, Max, Hugo and Ben

CONTENTS

Part Three
NURSERY DETAILS

FOREWORD

Nursery Style was very much a collaboration. It began because one of us (Annie Sloan) had spent much of her professional life designing, painting and decorating nurseries, and the other (Felicity Bryan) loved making everything from curtains and bean-bags to covers for bassinets. We were neighbors, with six children between us, so we decided to combine our different skills in a book which should cover the age range from birth to five. Our different approaches sparked many more ideas, making the book tremendous fun to write.

It has also been a collaboration with our children. When we embarked their ages ranged from not-yet-born to six – Felicity made the bassinet cover while in the hospital awaiting the arrival of her younger son, Ben. Over a year the children have, with varying degrees of enthusiasm, collaborated as their rooms have been transformed: Hugo's with a mural, Tom's with a sprayed sky, Henry's with painted shutters, Max's with jugglers and tumblers on his curtains and floor and a blackboard on the wall. Meanwhile Elaine Green created a Carl Larsson dream in Alice's little room with her enchanting stencils, and Anca Groves decked Ben's crib to make it the smartest in Oxfordshire. Five of our children appear as models in the book, as does the son of our excellent editor Tessa Strickland.

We owe a lot of thanks to our cooperative children and husbands, to David Evans for his ideas and help with painting, to Margie Fink who designed the Advent calendar and rag books for two small children in her charge, and to all the artists who have obligingly lent us their work (their names and addresses appear at the back of the book) – in particular Elaine Green and Anca Groves who created projects specifically for the book. In addition we were greatly helped by Merle Barrington, Mrs. Mansfield and the Bladon Primary School Infants Class, Helena Mercer, Susanna Fuller at Cogges Farm Museum, Witney, Susie Cartwright, Penny Honeyman, Karen Kennedy, Mrs. Polemis, Stella Vaines, Mr. and Mrs. Wickens and our photographers Fred Close, Ken Sandles, Peter Rauter, Ian Green, Graham Challifour and Graham Miller. Vanessa Hedley first interested Annie in design for children when Hippo Hall Children's Designs opened in London nine years ago.

Thank you also to Diana Levinson who had the original idea to commission the book, to Kate Parker who valiantly transformed our sketchy instructions into projects, to Bet Ayer for her lovely design, to Jenny de Gex for her diligent picture research and above all to our patient and encouraging editor Tessa Strickland.

Felicity Bryan   Annie Sloan

Part One

———————

BABIES' NURSERIES

Chapter One

PREPARING FOR YOUR BABY

Before your first baby is born you will have a lot of time – far too much, you may find – to think. Once he arrives you will have no time at all. So use the months before the birth constructively. Sit back and think about what your baby will need. Of course there are the immediate practical needs of a newborn – bassinet, changing mats and so on. But there is also the more important longer-term need, which we all have and never lose, for a place that is special to him.

The baby's room is the place where later he will build bricks, play house, dress dolls, grow seeds, act his first plays, read in peace or entertain friends, make treasured collections of shells, cars, toy animals. It is the one area of the house that is uniquely his and where, in years to come, adults enter on invitation alone. So you want to make the room as magical and attractive as possible. By the time a child is four or five he will begin to have strong views on what his room should be like. But for the time being you have *carte blanche*.

It is surprising how little trouble some people take over their children's rooms, decorating them, or not doing so, as if they were somehow temporary. Having a lovely room makes a child feel very special, and it is yet another manifestation of a parent's care. This does not mean that the room need be expensively equipped. This book is full of ideas for things you can buy or make at very little cost. The key is to have a clear idea of what effect you are aiming at, and a good eye for what will contribute to that effect.

In this book we give examples of different styles you might create. When a child is older his character may well dictate the style, but while he is still a tiny baby you need a different stepping-off point. It may be a piece of furniture such as a lovely old crib or rocking horse,

The centrepiece of this enchanting bedroom for a baby girl is the antique bassinet, restored by Anthea Moore Ede. The colours of the wallpaper and carpet have been chosen so as not to overpower the narrow space, while the full, feminine curtains enhance the romantic effect.

Everything is easily at hand in this baby's room. The waist-high work-top is ideal for changing tiny babies; above the chest of drawers is a storage space for diapers; the wall rails and hooks hold essential equipment.

which will prompt you to create a Victorian Nostalgic style, or a marvelous old quilt which will suggest to you American Country. Conversely, if you live in a very modern apartment with steel-framed windows and fittings, a cleaner, more contemporary style would be more appropriate. Whatever style you choose, it is important that the room should marry well with the rest of the house. It is also worth remembering that you do not need to create a total "look" all at once. The room may begin as something quite simple, and you can make changes as the years go by and your child develops stronger views on his surroundings. (There are few things more exciting for a child of four than helping his father or mother to create a mural of a tree on his nursery wall using simple potato prints.) In this way, you will also be able to control the amount of money you spend on your child's room. Don't go overboard and spend huge amounts on lace and frills for a new baby unless you can afford to redecorate after the first year. Make lasting items such as sturdy cribs/beds and practical storage areas your main priority, and then build around these following the suggestions given in Parts Two and Three.

BABY'S FIRST ROOM

Although the newborn may sleep in your room at night for the first few months, he will take his daytime naps in his own room and later sleep there at night too. Ideally, therefore, it should be close to your bedroom. The baby's room may also be the place where all the bathing and cleaning up will take place, so if possible it should be near the bathroom. If this is not possible, think of installing a sink, preferably hidden in a closet or behind a screen.

You will spend a lot of time in this room, so it should be comfortable, light and warm. Opt for light, cheerful colors, avoiding dark or garish ones. Steer clear of stereotypes: an all-pink room for a girl can look awfully sugary, and blue on its own is quite a cold color unless it is cheered up with warm whites, yellows or reds. It seems silly to begin with a sexist approach to your baby's room. The outside world will influence the child all too soon. Girls may not want flowers and frills, and boys may find soldiers in bright colours limiting as a backdrop to imaginative play.

The floor will be spilled on a lot, so select a practical mottled or patterned carpet which won't show stains. If you have a wooden or parquet floor invest in a large rug (firmly fixed so that it won't slip about or trip toddlers up) for the first few years. When choosing curtains, remember that to keep the room dark at nap time they should be lined. Make them short, for toddlers can pull down floor-length curtains and will stain them with grubby fingers.

Babies lead to quantities of clutter, so plan practical storage space with shelves, cabinets and drawers which can later be used for toys, books and clothes. You may need both a crib and a cradle, though some babies move

This classic lacy cradle is of a kind we associate with Victorian royal babies. It still looks enchanting today, and can be decked with practical, washable cotton fabrics.

straight from their bassinet to a crib. Other essentials are a changing table with mat, a comfortable chair to sit in while you feed the baby, a bath, perhaps a cart on which

13

This light and airy room is further enhanced by curtains, bedlinen and accessories in delicately tinted eyelet. These are all made by Simplantex, who produce a complete range of co-ordinated nursery fabrics and accessories.

you can keep the bath and bath things, airtight buckets for diapers, a washable play rug and perhaps a play pen. Some babies will not be left in play pens, and in fact some doctors advise against using them. But many babies seem perfectly happy in them and they are a boon to harassed parents trying to look after several children at once.

If you have the space it is sensible to include a bed in this room. The baby can graduate to it when he is older, and you will meanwhile find it a boon when dressing him. It will also be useful if he is unwell and you have to stay with him at night. The furniture in the room must all be sturdy – and beware of dangerous sharp edges.

A bassinet is a must. You can either buy a ready-lined bassinet or, if you prefer, buy the basket only and make the lining yourself (see p. 20). When selecting the cotton for the lining, buy some extra material so that you can make laundry bags, lined baskets for storage, diaper stackers and traveling bags in the same fabric. Small babies are very portable, and it is fun to go visiting with them if you are sensibly equipped. Simple traveling bags consisting of a padded changing mat, with handles and pockets in the side for holding diapers, cotton wool, feeding bottles, etc., can be purchased in the children's departments of many stores and are enormously useful. If you make one of these bags yourself you can use the same fabric to run up a few rectangular bags with drawstrings in which to put clutter when traveling. These can later be useful as shoe bags.

Changing a baby can be a messy job, so you might keep a changing apron in the baby's room. You could make this in a co-ordinating fabric, with useful large pockets. Incidentally, in the early months it is a help if your everyday clothes have pockets large enough to hold a spare diaper or a bottle.

For the first few months of life, babies have no strength in their necks, and a towel with a small hood over one corner will provide valuable extra support. Towels with hoods are now sold in the children's departments of many stores. Alternatively, you can make your own quite easily by following the instructions on p. 92.

OPPOSITE: Accessories for a new baby: above – a layette with bassinet, towel and sheets; (l to r) – painted baskets for cotton wool and creams; a Beatrix Potter fabric traveling basket with a diaper changer that zips up into a bag; a contemporary English willow bassinet.

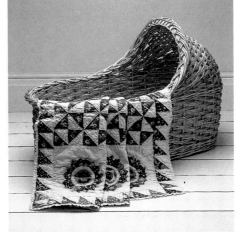

CELEBRATING YOUR BABY

Throughout the world, and in numerous different societies and religions, there are ceremonies in which a new child is presented to his community and family. These often take the form of a naming ceremony, which is usually accompanied by a celebratory party, and presents are given to the baby. In many societies naming ceremonies are particularly important, as they establish the legitimacy of the baby.

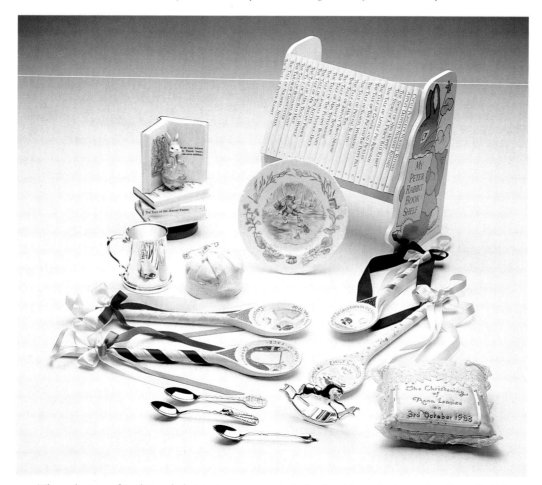

This selection of traditional christening presents includes (looking clockwise) *a Peter Rabbit bookcase with a set of Beatrix Potter books; a Jeremy Fisher plate; celebration spoons painted with the name of the child, the date of birth and ribbons to hang the spoons; a silk and lace christening cushion with the child's name and date of birth; a silver rocking horse; solid silver spoons with decorated ends; a silver-plated spoon with a Beatrix Potter decoration on the end; a silver-plated christening mug with engraved Beatrix Potter figures; a pin cushion; and a Peter Rabbit china music box.*

The Christian version is usually a christening, though if the parents choose not to have their child christened there can be a service of thanksgiving and blessing for the birth of the child. The Baptists and Pentecostal churches who have adult baptism hold dedication services for the birth of a child. In Jewish society a party is given after the circumcision of a boy or the naming of a girl. The Hindus have a ceremony where a sacred thread is put around the body of a new baby boy. The prevalence of these ceremonies shows that we all have a need to have our babies recognized by society, as well as a longing to celebrate each new arrival.

So whether you observe a particular religion or not, you will find that giving a party to celebrate your child and present him to your friends will be a very enriching experience for everyone. Non-believers also sometimes nominate "godparents" or sponsors.

Traditionally, christening presents were often made of silver. Silver apostle spoons were popular in eighteenth-century England, as were silver mugs and bowls, and silver presents are still given today. But nowadays a child is equally likely to receive a beautiful book, a special piece of china or pottery, or some small piece of furniture.

You can make some lovely naming presents or christening presents yourself. Think of something which will last and be a reminder of an important day. Name pictures are a fine idea, and children enjoy them enormously – you can paint them or embroider the names on a sampler. Name cushions can be made easily with appliqué or embroidery. A painted box is another good and lasting idea, and a beautiful painted chair with a child's name on it should last for generations. Ceramic paints from arts and crafts shops can be used directly on to plates. Paint the child's name, date of birth and perhaps birthweight. Decorate simply, with dots and dashes.

Robert Young has painted this christening box in a traditional American primitive style. The child's name is painted on the lid. The paint colors are chalky blues and greens with imitation wood grain borders.

A handpainted name picture, a Tweedledum pottery teapot, cut-out wooden animal with letter and a fabric appliquéd ABC book. These would all make excellent and unusual christening presents.

SAFETY

The world is full of potential dangers to a baby or a small child, so make it your business to ensure that your home, and the baby's room in particular, is as safe as possible. As a general principle, think of safety not just from the point of view of the *intended* use of the toys, furniture and other equipment in your house, but of their misuse also. Flimsy furniture will not withstand the mountaineering attempts of a toddler; curtain cords, crib bumper ties and other lengths of thin cord that could strangle a child should be replaced or shortened to a length which is not hazardous; bedding and other materials, if they are loosely woven, can be pulled apart and the fibers swallowed. But forewarned is forearmed: you will minimize the risk of danger to your baby if you child-proof your home before his arrival. So consider everything that your baby might use or abuse and remove/replace any dangerous items. The following safety precautions should all be observed.

ELECTRICITY

A small baby will chew anything, so don't have any electric cords within reach, and don't let them run across the floor to be tripped over. Avoid table lamps which could be pulled off the table. Avoid using electric kettles or irons in the baby's room. Don't use electric fires with exposed elements. If possible, have electric outlets high up where a toddler cannot reach. Alternatively, you can install special shuttered electric sockets which open only when a plug is put in. Failing this, cover all electric sockets with plastic socket covers.

PLASTIC BAGS

These hold a great fascination for babies. Remember that a child can smother if he puts his head in an airtight bag, so keep plastic diaper bucket liners and other plastic bags well out of reach.

FURNITURE

All furniture should have rounded edges so that a child cannot hurt himself badly when falling. It must not be top-heavy, otherwise it may fall on the child, and it must be stable even when it is used during rough-and-tumble games. Glass-topped tables are not safe for small children, nor are ornamental tables with floor-length covers that can be pulled off, bringing the ornaments with them.

Be sure that your crib is safe. If you buy a new crib, make sure it has a safety standard label. Antique cribs often have bars so wide apart that a child could get his head stuck between them. If you want to use such a crib, line it carefully with well-padded material. Be sure you have a modern safety mattress, and avoid using pillows as they can cause suffocation. A toddler will move to a bed at around the age of two. Choose a strong bed with a firm mattress. Do not introduce bunk beds until the child is at least five: younger children can easily fall out.

WATER

Remember that a small baby can drown in a couple of inches of water, so never leave an unemptied bath or bucket of water about. Hot water can burn a baby's sensitive skin, so turn hot water taps off tightly. If you have an electric kettle, keep it on a safe, stable surface where it cannot be knocked over and where the cord cannot be reached.

POISONS

Many family medicines can be fatal in large doses, so make sure that all medicines are kept in a locked cabinet placed well out of reach of your child. Remember that many other fluids can also be harmful to young children, so keep disinfectant, baby shampoo and bottle sterilizing equipment well out of the range of exploring hands.

STAIRS

A bad fall downstairs can injure a person of any age. Install safety gates if your house has stairs, and in particular if your baby's nursery is immediately at the top of a flight of stairs.

FIRES

Avoid open fires. If you choose to have one, you should buy a large fireguard of the type which can be attached safely to the wall on either side of the fireplace and store matches and firelighters in a safe place well away from the fire and preferably in a different room. Make sure that the bed and chair are not made of foam, which gives out poisonous fumes in the event of a fire. Make sure that none of the baby's clothes or bedding are made of synthetic fibers, which might catch fire easily.

WINDOWS

A toddler can very easily climb up and fall out of a window, so be sure to install safety catches which limit the amount a window can be opened. Alter-natively, you can buy bars to be temporarily fixed inside or outside the window, or install plantation shutters, which can have their slats opened like Venetian blinds but at the same time eliminate the danger of falls.

LEAD POISONING

Most modern paints do not contain dangerous amounts of lead. However, the paintwork on old toys and furniture may well do so. For this reason you must be enormously careful, when your baby is teething, to see that he does not chew painted objects unless the toys carry specific safety labels. When removing old paint do not use blowtorches in the vicinity of your baby's room, as they cause toxic fumes. Do not rub down with sandpaper or use an electric sander or you will fill the air with lead dust.

TOYS

Every year new toys come on to the market and have subsequently to be withdrawn after reports of accidents. Look before you buy: test toys to make sure they cannot be pulled apart to reveal nails or sharp edges, and check that they have no parts small enough to be swallowed. Double-check old toys for signs of rust or splintered wood, and don't buy new ones unless they have an approved safety label.

ANIMALS

Never allow cats or dogs in the baby's room. If you keep cats or if there are cats in your neighborhood, always put a cat net over the basket or pram when a baby is sleeping, whether outdoors or in.

LINING A BASSINET

The following instructions are for the lining and coverlet of a basket measuring 33 in/83 cm at the longest point, 17 in/42 cm at the widest point, and 9 in/22 cm deep, with a base measuring 26 in/65 cm × 14 in/36 cm. Measure your basket and allow more fabric if necessary. Any pretty cotton fabric with not too large a design will do. You can use ready-quilted cotton (no wadding necessary), especially for a winter baby, though the selection of quilted fabrics available is quite limited.

MATERIALS
- For basket lining and coverlet: $5\frac{1}{2}$ yd/5 m of fabric 36 in/90 cm wide (you will need less material for a wider fabric and/or if you opt for contrasting frills and ribbons – see below)
- For lining/coverlet frills and ribbons, if using contrasting fabric: $3\frac{1}{4}$ yd/$2\frac{3}{4}$ m of fabric 36 in/90 cm wide
- $3\frac{1}{3}$ yd/3 m of 4-oz wadding
- Piece of foam $1\frac{1}{2}$ in/4 cm deep, cut to fit base of basket (or two or three layers of wadding)
- Waterproof sheeting to cover mattress
- Press studs
- Ribbons (fabric allowance included above)
- Tracing paper
- Pencil
- Scissors
- Needles
- Pins
- Thread

PATTERN
Bassinets vary in size, so you must make your own pattern with tracing paper. Usually the basket is higher at the end where the baby's head will lie.
1 Set the basket on the tracing paper and draw around it to make an outline to be used for the base of the lining and for the coverlet. Place the cut shape inside the basket and mark $\frac{5}{8}$ in/1.5 cm from the edge with a pen to indicate the seam line.
2 Place tracing paper to cover the inner sides of the basket, cutting one piece for the head section (A) and two other pieces for the sides (B and C). (See diagram i.) Allow $\frac{5}{8}$ in/1.5 cm around each section for the seams and a further 2 in/5 cm at the top for the lining to hang slightly over the edge of the basket.
3 To make facings for the gaps for the handles to come through, measure each handle from one outside edge to the other (15 in/37 cm for our basket) and add an extra $\frac{7}{8}$ in/2 cm at each end. Cut some paper this length (i.e. $16\frac{1}{2}$ in/41 cm for our basket) and 2 in/5 cm wide.
4 Cut paper for 4 ribbon lengths. Ours are $1\frac{1}{2}$ in/4 cm wide by 20 in/50 cm long, but you can make them wider and longer.

20

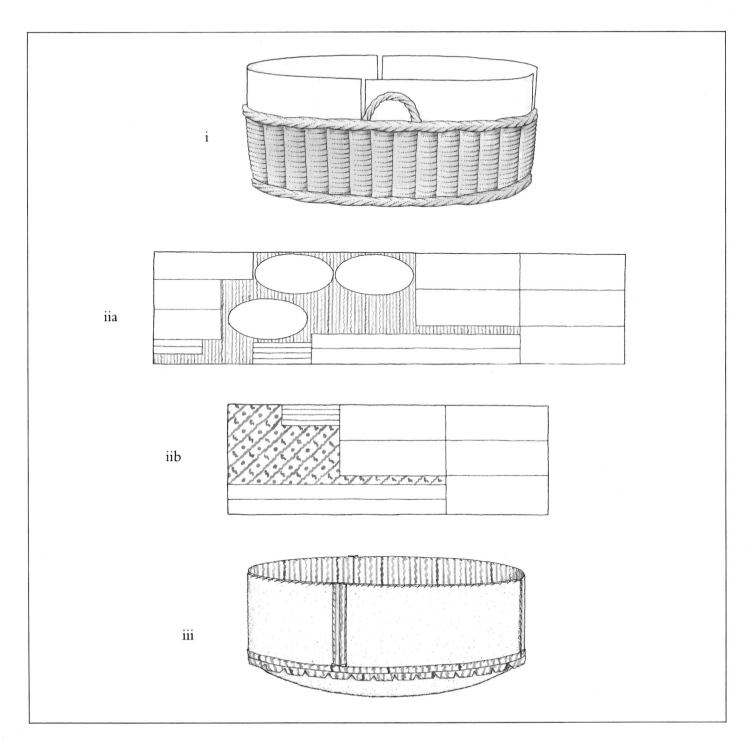

i

iia

iib

iii

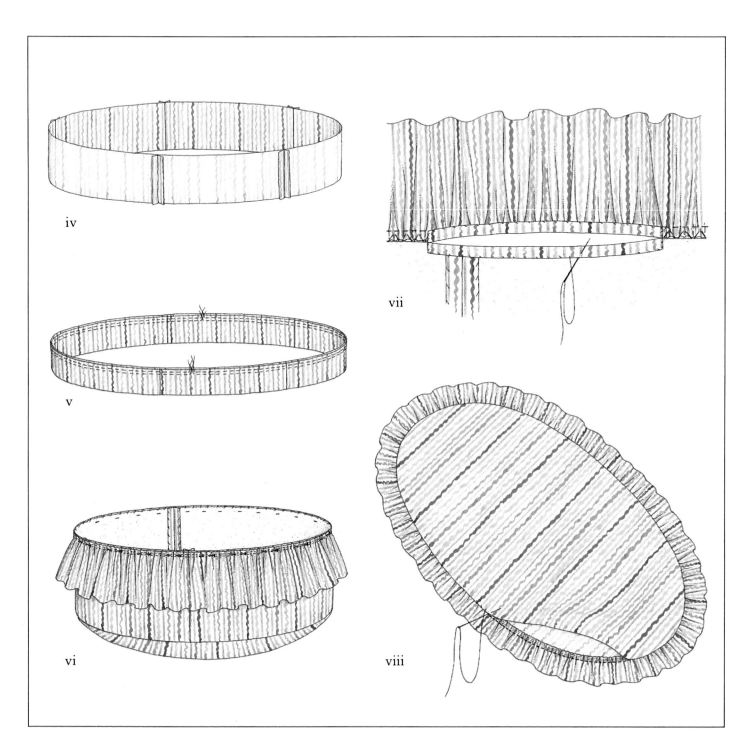

iv

v

vi

vii

viii

22

5 Cut paper for a deep frill. If 36 in/90 cm width fabric is used, you will need to cut 5 lengths 36 in/90 cm × 12 in/30 cm which, when sewn together, will form a frill 180 in/450 cm long (or 176 in/440 cm, allowing for seams).

6 For the coverlet frill, cut paper twice the circumference by 5 in/12 cm deep. The pattern for the lining frill can be cut in sections.

MAKING UP

1 Lay out your pattern pieces on the fabric, remembering that you will need to cut out three "base" pieces – one for the lining base and two for each side of the coverlet – and two pieces for the handle hole facings. (See diagram ii for layouts.)

2 Cut out the wadding, using the pattern pieces for the sides and base, and cutting an extra "base" piece to line the coverlet.

3 Tack the wadding to the fabric for the base and side pieces and oversew each section. Sew the side pieces together, fabric inwards, and press the seams open. Pin the sides to the base section and, after making sure that it fits the basket well, sew together and press the seams. (See diagram iii.)

4 *Frill*: Oversew each section along the side to be joined. Join each piece end to end and sew together to form a complete loop; press the seams open. Fold the "loop" in half along its length (raw edges of seams inwards) and press. Sew two parallel rows of gathering stitches along the side of the loop where the two edges meet, then pull up the stitching and pin evenly round the top of the lining with the right side of the lining fabric facing the frill, adjusting the gathering threads to fit. Machine together and oversew the seam before pressing. (See diagrams iv–vi.)

5 *Handle facings*: Place the lining back in the basket and mark clearly the position of the basket handles. Tack each facing to the inside of the lining and frill along a line from the outside of the basket handles (see illustration). Sew two parallel lines approximately 1 in/2 cm apart and joining just beyond the point where each side of the handle will pass through, as if making a giant buttonhole. Cut along the center of the lines to create the "buttonhole." Turn the binding fabric in, and hem the edges neatly to the inside of the lining and frill. (See diagram vii.)

6 *Accessories*: Attach snaps as shown in the illustration. To make the ribbons, fold each piece of fabric in half, press and pin together, and sew along three sides leaving a gap along one short edge. Turn inside out, press, and hem open edge. Attach the ribbons as shown in the illustration.

7 *Coverlet*: To make the frill, cut out the fabric using the pattern described above and make up following the instructions for the lining frill. Gather the frill and pin it around the top side of one piece of the coverlet fabric, right sides of fabric facing in. Sew together.

Tack the wadding to the underside of the second piece of coverlet fabric. Pin both sections together, right sides of fabric together and frill tucked inside, and machine around the edge leaving a few inches open so you can turn the coverlet inside out. Once turned, hem the hole and press. (See diagram viii.)

8 *Mattress*: Using the "base" pattern, cut out two sections of waterproof sheeting, remembering to allow $\frac{5}{8}$ in/1.5 cm for seams. Pin together and sew around the edge, leaving a gap for turning inside out. Turn, fill with the sponge or wadding (cut out from the "base" pattern), and sew up the gap.

The Blue Bird – Children Recounting Their Adventures, *by Frederick Cayley Robinson.*

Part Two

NURSERY STYLES

Chapter Two

NURSERIES OF THE PAST

It has been said that childhood is a twentieth-century invention. Certainly the idea of childhood as a separate state, with its own privileges and traditions, is comparatively new. And the concept of play as a creative occupation in itself is very recent indeed. Family portraits up to the nineteenth century depict children as miniature adults dressed just like their parents. Not until the turn of this century were they dressed in garments really suited to children's occupations.

It is significant that nobody thought of publishing books specially written for children until the mid eighteenth century. At this time Jean-Jacques Rousseau was scandalizing many parents with his writings, advocating a much more free approach to the upbringing of children who, he wrote, must no longer be constrained and molded to be mirror images of their parents. Later in the nineteenth century, writers such as Lewis Carroll did a lot to romanticize the idea of the child with her own magic world of innocence separate from that of adults.

Our knowledge of how children lived in the past is generally restricted to the children of well-to-do parents, who could write and leave a record of their doings. We know that in some rich households from the sixteenth century in England there were separate nurseries. But on the whole families in Britain, Europe and America lived very much *en famille*. It was only in nineteenth-century Britain that the classic nursery evolved.

THE HEYDAY OF THE NURSERY

In Victorian Britain – a thrusting society with many newly-rich families – nurseries became a regular feature of all self-respecting middle-class households. Very few English dolls' houses included nurseries until the

This magnificent Victorian gothic revival nursery at Cardiff Castle was created by the architect William Burges. The frieze is made of hand-painted tiles showing scenes and characters from the tales of Hans Christian Andersen, the brothers Grimm and The Arabian Nights.

The classic mid nineteenth-century day nursery at Erddig, complete with a sturdy mahogany table for meals and lessons. The toy collection is typical of the time, and the rocking horse is of the early variety, set on simple rockers.

A portrait of William Brooke, 10th Earl Cobham, with his Family, attributed to the Master of the Countess of Warwick (around 1560–70).

This deserted room at Calke Abbey in Derbyshire has all the trappings of a once busy nursery complete with magnificent old rocking horse, horses on wheels and a splendid dolls' house.

nineteenth century. The large Victorian house would have two: a day nursery and a night nursery. In the day nursery, the antecedent of the modern playroom, the children took their meals and lessons and played, and they slept in the night nursery. Many servants and nurserymaids were employed, under the stern command of Nanny. Children were brought downstairs to their parents after tea, but otherwise led lives extraordinarily separate from their mothers and fathers.

Not until the late nineteenth century was it suggested that nurseries should be at all attractive. The typical day nursery was a big room at the top of the house and contained a large toy cabinet, a cabinet for clothes and a cabinet for the nursery crockery. None of this furniture would have been selected with children in mind, and it probably comprised cast-offs from the rest of the house.

While older children slept in the night nursery, there would probably be a cradle for the smallest child in the day nursery. A fire would blaze in the large fireplace, its purpose not just to heat the room but to air the linen, which was hung over a high, brass-edged fender, secured to the wall by hooks. By the fire was Nanny's chair, and in the center of the room was a substantial table for meals, lessons and games; there might also be a miniature table and chairs for smaller children to use. The two toys invariably visible were a dolls' house and a rocking horse. Screens covered with cut-out scraps, as well as being attractive, had the very real practical purpose of keeping out drafts.

Life in the nursery had its own routine. After breakfast – brought up many flights of stairs from the kitchen – came toilet training. A child would first be put on the toilet at one month and would be toilet-trained by a year. Then, in mid morning, it would be out for a walk, rain or shine. Next a plain lunch, then, after more toilet training, a nap. The routine continued for the rest of the day, including a visit to the parents after tea. The mother would drop in on nursery functions as she chose.

Though these nurseries of the past were plain places, they seem from many accounts to have been well stocked with toys. Some toys, hobby horses for example, go back many centuries, as do toy soldiers, hoops, paper windmills, kites and stilts. Dolls were called babies until the mid eighteenth century, and early dolls' houses were called baby houses. Dolls became very popular in the nineteenth century, while teddy bears, named after Theodore Roosevelt, were an invention of the early twentieth century.

At the turn of this century, wallpaper, rugs and pictures designed specially for nurseries at last began to appear. Walter Crane's wallpapers, with animals, birds and fairytale figures, and Kate Greenaway's designs, with idealized children, were particularly popular and very much set the tone for children's friezes of today.

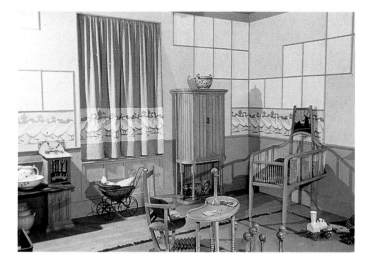

CHILDREN'S FURNITURE

Furniture has been made specially for children for many centuries but, with the exception of cribs, high chairs and baby walkers, it tended until recently to be adult furniture in miniature. By far the most common articles of antique childhood furniture are cribs and chairs. Baby walkers also made an early appearance. Most of the children's furniture which survives to this day dates from the sixteenth century onwards. Some beautiful American children's furniture survives from the eighteenth and nineteenth centuries; the trouble that was taken with little bureaus, chairs and other items may reflect the fact that in the freer society of America, where children were seen and heard around the house, the furniture was more likely to be on show in the adult part of the house.

Until the mid eighteenth century, newborn babies in England and Europe were literally bound up in swaddling clothes in their cradles and then covered with blankets. There were instances of suffocation from too much bedding, but the practice of swaddling persisted much later in some parts of Europe. Once out of swaddling clothes, both boys and girls were dressed in skirts, the boys finally being put into breeches at six.

The cradles of the rich have always been very dressed up, but the standard oak rocking cradle common in seventeenth-century England could be quite plain. Very similar cradles, often made of pine, are found in America.

This fascinating art deco room is a very arch reconstruction by Cecil Beaton of a nursery of 1901 which must have seemed very daring at the time. Beaton recreated the room for the Ideal Home Exhibition in 1958. The darker painted dado area is a practical idea, and the charming duck theme extends at chair height to the curtains. The inlaid furniture which echoes the duck theme is exquisitely made.

This simple English oak rocking cradle probably dates from the seventeenth century, though the practical design continued for a long time and was transported to America. Its lack of decoration suggests that it belonged to a humble family or perhaps to Puritans.

Willow cradles, still made today (see p. 65), have been used for centuries, and so have swinging cradles made in wood and later in ironwork or in canework and mahogany (see p. 36).

Baby walkers have been used since the Middle Ages, and many survive. Sometimes they included a play table, as many modern ones do. Playpens were also a feature of eighteenth- and nineteenth-century life.

Many children's chairs, both high and low, can be found from the Middle Ages onwards. They all tend to be in the same style as the adult chairs of the period. It is only in the late nineteenth century that we begin to see some charming chairs that were designed specially for children, echoing a whole new attitude to nurseries and nursery life.

Room Sets from Sotheby's Exhibition of Childhood, 1988

TOP: The rocking horse is probably the first ever made. It was given to King Charles I when he was a child, in about 1610. The oak high chairs are early seventeenth century. The elm baby walker was made in about 1700. The other seventeenth-century pieces are small replicas of adult furniture.

BOTTOM: A classic late eighteenth-century wooden baby walker on wooden casters and mid seventeenth-century carved oak cradle in the North Country English style. The elaborate carved high chair and the oak and leather high chair, a replica of what the adults would have used, are both seventeenth century.

OPPOSITE: A collection of nineteenth- and twentieth-century furniture. The painted Windsor-style armchair with carved village folk is dated 1916. The highchair in the corner is a rare yew Windsor weighing and exercise chair.

Chapter Three

VICTORIAN NOSTALGIC

Though the real Victorian nursery was generally quite a stark room, our image of it is bathed in nostalgia and based much more on the nurseries of the late Victorian and Edwardian era. Only then did nurseries begin to be pretty, with all the lace and frills and flounces, ribbons and bows, pretty chintz patterns and soft colors which some of the smartest interior design shops still emulate today.

It is not difficult to achieve this nostalgic look. You can start by picking up old bits of furniture which look the part at quite low prices. Don't struggle slavishly to recreate an exact copy of a Victorian nursery. Rather, aim to create a mood of old-world aristocratic luxury by using the aspects of Victoriana which suit today's homes.

First decide how you want to break up your wall space. The Victorians often divided their walls horizontally. From the floor to about waist height was the dado area which was often papered with anaglypta, a heavy, embossed wallpaper which is still sold today and which can be painted with gloss, making it easily washable. Above the dado rail was either wallpaper or paint, extending up to the frieze and/or picture rail. Above that would be a plain paint color. Colors were rich and deep and polychromatic. The Victorians did not enjoy primary colors but favored rather muddy blues and greens and reds.

Obviously you don't want a nursery that looks dark and gloomy – lighter colors, whether they are plain or patterned, will create a brighter, happier ambience. The Victorians did not consciously use paint techniques such as ragging, sponging and dragging; but the texture of nineteenth-century paint mixes tended to create a "dragged" look. So these techniques look well in Victorian homes today, and if you select the right colors you can

The dark-framed, old-fashioned pictures, button-backed chair, wrought iron crib, old-fashioned quilts and pretty wallpaper all help to give this nursery a Victorian feel. The sides of an old crib such as this should be reinforced as the width of the bars makes them unsafe for children.

Here, at Arlington Court, Devon, we see a classic Victorian nursery complete with wicker and mahogany rocking cradle and a fender around the fire for drying clothes.

achieve a very warm, welcoming atmosphere. The Victorians began to use wallpaper in nurseries towards the end of the nineteenth century. If you want a Victorian-style wallpaper, choose small, old-fashioned floral designs or perhaps a Regency stripe. Friezes could show childhood scenes from Kate Greenaway or, in a boy's room, soldiers and sailors. Silhouettes were popular in the Victorian period, and you could make a silhouette frieze or picture as described on p. 44.

Samplers go back many centuries, but the Victorians particularly liked them. Quite small children would be put to making a sampler. You can easily make one for your child, either designing your own pattern or buying one of the many kits that are available. You can pick up pretty old prints quite easily, or even cut out and frame pages from one of the many Kate Greenaway books which are still published. Frames look best in varnished

wood in rich dark colors, or in more ornate silver or brass if you are lucky enough to have them.

The floor of a Victorian nursery would probably have had polished boards, with large patterned rugs in traditional Persian styles or made in needlepoint or tapestry. If you decide to use carpet, choose subdued colors, tending towards dark, with rugs scattered on top.

Curtains used to be long, though this is very impractical for children, and were awash with flounces, frills and swags. For fabrics, old-fashioned prints of childhood scenes can again be used, or small-flowered chintz edged with lace or frills. Velvet was very popular with the Victorians, and it can look lovely combined with lace. Muslin and lace were also used in day nurseries, though they are no good for keeping out the light. Queen Victoria loved the Scottish Highlands, and the Victorians were very keen on tartan. Tartan ribbons look

VICTORIAN WALL DECORATIONS

TOP: Making silhouettes was a favorite pastime for ladies of leisure in the Regency and Victorian periods. BOTTOM (l to r): An embroidered sampler, worked predominantly in silks, made by Ann Walsell in 1825; a nursery wallpaper designed by Kate Greenaway in 1893 (wallpaper was mass-produced from the 1840s and by the end of the century could be seen in all middle-class homes); another embroidered sampler made by Helen Peggs, c1850.
(There are contemporary kits available for samplers.)

particularly attractive with white or cream cotton. Tartan rugs and trimmings look good in boys' or girls' rooms.

Pretty quilts were very popular in Victorian times, either in plain quilting or in a combination of patchwork and quilting. You can pick up old quilts at high prices but you can also make them yourself, perhaps personalizing them with your baby's initials. Once out of his crib, a Victorian child would move to a bed with a big puffy feather-filled eiderdown covered in cotton with either a paisley or a floral design. Sheets and pillows would be white and might be edged with lace or embroidered, perhaps with a monogram.

Old cribs and cradles are expensive and hard to come by, unless you are lucky, and they do not always meet modern standards of safety. For instance, be sure that the bars of a crib are not so wide apart that a child can stick his head through. If they are too wide apart you will have to line the crib with quilted fabric for safety. Rocking cradles, made of wood, painted iron or painted basket-work, look very appropriate in a Victorian-style room. You can make your own cradle trimmings, for example the traditional white lacy hood which we associate with royal babies. Brass-topped bedsteads were common in Victorian and Edwardian England, and many cribs were painted white with brass knobs. Mahogany and darker woods were also fashionable. Furniture was sometimes painted, using delicate colors. It was also fashionable to paint little garlands of flowers, particularly in the center of a table or on the top of a chest of drawers.

The atmosphere of the best Victorian houses was one of elegant clutter. The walls were scattered with pictures, screens were covered with decorative scraps which both children and adults collected, ornaments were everywhere. Obviously, it is important to keep ornaments out of the way of small children, so they should be restricted to areas high up where curious hands cannot reach. It is easy to cover a screen: you can use authentic-looking period scraps, which are still made today, like Victorian postcards or old-fashioned wrapping paper. Scraps can also be used on cheap furniture and boxes to achieve a delightful effect.

Dolls' houses and rocking horses featured in Victorian nurseries. Boys often collected tin soldiers and painted wooden soldiers and, later, elaborate train sets. Today you can buy contemporary wooden toys which fit the bill and make charming ornaments. The nineteenth century was also the great age of the doll. Victorian dolls at last began to look like children, and were usually equipped with little wooden rocking cradles.

This collage screen is typical of the many screens which were decorated in the nineteenth century. Screens served a very real purpose of stopping drafts, but they became works of art when decorated with these special scraps.

These contemporary painted wooden toys are made in very much the Boys' Own tradition which we associate with the period before the First World War, when soldierly qualities were glorified.

The Jubilee Quilt was made by children at a Yorkshire Sunday school to celebrate Queen Victoria's Diamond Jubilee in 1897. As well as the initials of the queen embroidered in golden yellow with crowns, the children have embroidered their own initials and the names of their families. It is all hand-made in red and white rough cotton.

39

VICTORIAN NOSTALGIC (BOYS)

VICTORIAN NOSTALGIC (GIRLS)

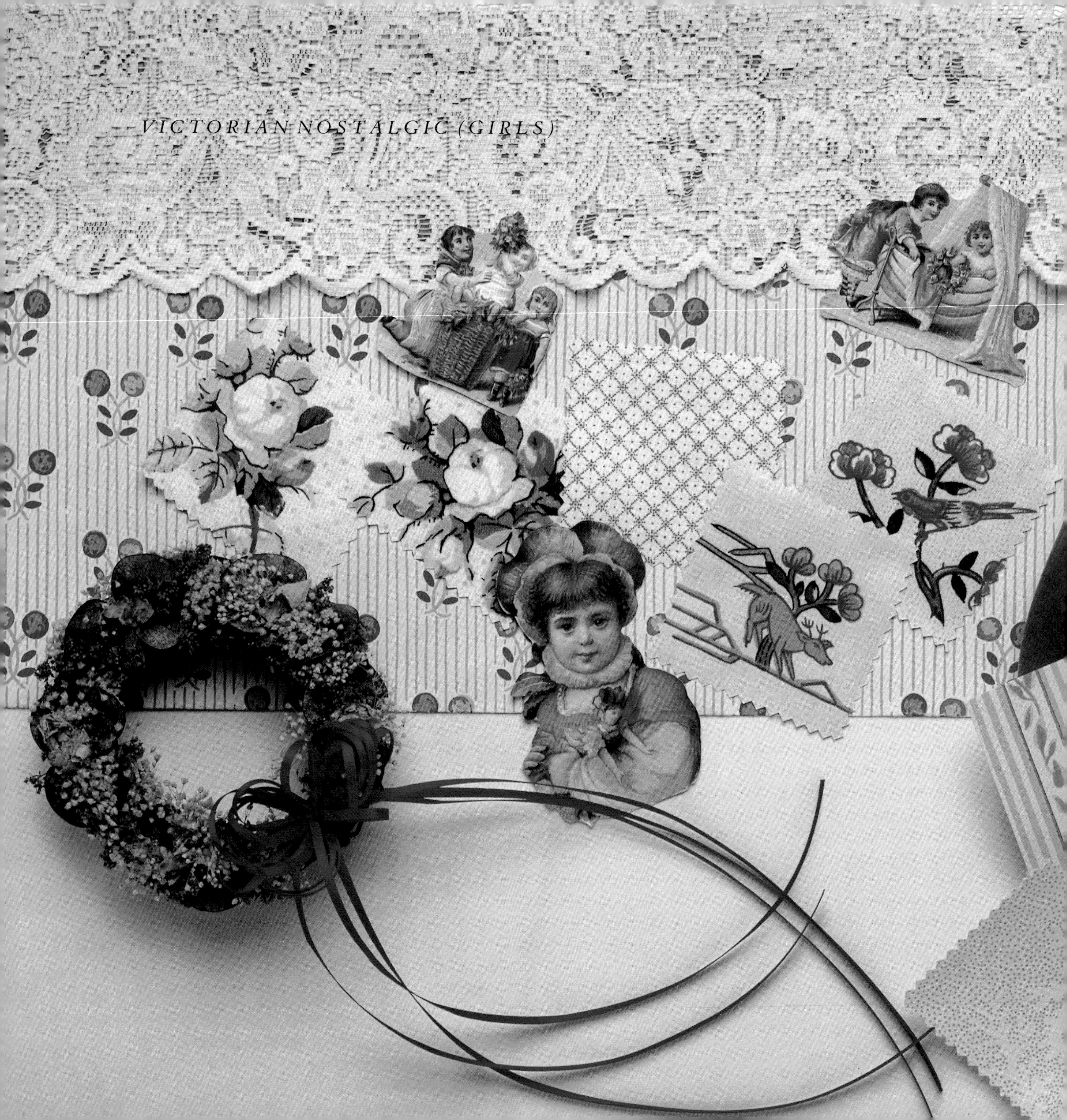

DESIGNING A SILHOUETTE FRIEZE

Cutting silhouettes was a popular pastime in the Regency and Victorian eras. The silhouettes were either used as friezes or mounted, framed and hung.

The silhouette shown here is a Victorian example. Nineteenth-century silhouettes often depicted group scenes or told a story, but you can make a much more simple one for a nursery frieze by using a repeating motif. The most common color for silhouettes is black, but you can use brighter colours. Some attractive combinations are: dark green silhouette paper against a pale green wall; mid-blue against cream; pastels against white or off-white.

MATERIALS
- Graph paper
- Pencil
- Ruler
- Tracing paper
- Scrap paper
- Thick, colored art paper for cutting the silhouette. The quantity you need will depend on the measurements of your room. Before you buy the paper, measure the width of your design and the total length of your frieze to calculate how many sheets of paper you will need.
- Scissors
- Spray adhesive
- Spray mount glue
- Step-ladder

METHOD
1 Make sure the wall surfaces are completely smooth before you start, as any bumps or notches will show through the silhouette paper. Silhouettes are best applied to matte paint or wallpaper surfaces. Avoid gloss paints and shiny wall surfaces, as you will have difficulty making the silhouette adhere to them.
2 To calculate the best size and position for your frieze, measure each wall and draw experimental designs on paper. Make thumbnail sketches of each wall, taking into account the size and position of doors, windows and any piece of furniture that stands against the wall. The best position for your frieze will depend on the proportions of your room; if you want to lower a high ceiling, place the frieze slightly lower down than you would for a low ceiling (see diagram i).
3 When you have decided where your frieze will look best, measure the walls carefully and put regular pencil marks to indicate the lower border of the frieze. These will act as guidelines for you when you glue the silhouette to the wall.
4 To make a silhouette with a repeating, mirror-image motif, you need an interlinking design like the traditional paper-dolly chain (see diagram ii). Experiment with different figures and shapes on scrap paper until you arrive at a design with a simple, clean outline.

5 Cut out your final design on tracing paper.

6 Cut each sheet of silhouette paper into strips that correspond to the height of your design. If you are working from a roll of paper, you will also need to cut it into manageable lengths; otherwise the design will tear when you try to glue it to the wall.

7 Take the first strip and fold it into a series of pleats that correspond to the width of your design.

8 Using a light spray adhesive, position your tracing on the uppermost fold of the silhouette paper and carefully cut around it, through all the pleats.

9 Peel off the tracing paper and repeat the folding and cutting process on successive strips until your frieze is complete.

10 Spread out some old newspaper on the floor or work surface and apply glue to the reverse side of the silhouette. Use the spray mount to spray on the glue.

11 Using a step-ladder if necessary, lift the silhouette up carefully and press it against the walls, following your pencil guide lines. Start in the centre of each wall and work outwards, section by section.

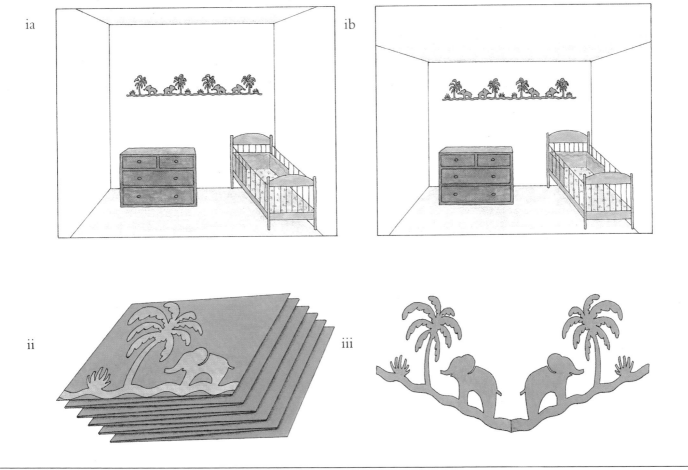

Chapter Four

AMERICAN COUNTRY STYLE

This style embraces everything from the classic American Colonial to the much rougher, handmade styles of the pioneers of the American West. American traditional furniture and decoration owe a great deal to their European antecedents, but have a vibrancy and warmth about them that are uniquely American. The exciting use of stencils for walls, furniture and bed covers, the simple prints, hooked rugs, carved ornaments, primitive paintings and, above all, the marvelous patchwork and appliqué quilts and cushions of America make this a delightful and extremely practical style for a child's room.

Wallpapers are out. The early pioneers could not afford or easily obtain expensive imported wallpapers, and, with interiors that often consisted of plain wood or plaster, they evolved a style of painted and stenciled walls which, while entirely American, had its roots particularly in Swedish and German folk art. Itinerant painters moved from house to house with their paints and stencil kits, decorating the walls. The designs were often symbolic: popular motifs included pineapples for hospitality, hearts and bells for joy, and bowls and baskets of fruit, signifying plenty.

Walls were sometimes painted a plain pastel color or white and then decorated with a stenciled border around the top, above the skirting board and around the doors and windows and any other architectural feature. On the least important wall there might be a simple repeated motif, while around the main chimney breast at the center of the room there was a more elaborate design. Some of these designs were symbolic patterns; others took the form of a mural. The stencil color was applied flat and was never shaded. The most widely used colors for stenciling and painting were yellow, green, an earthy

This nursery in a house on Long Island, complete with its exposed beams and log cabin look, has many of the features of American Country but a completely fresh contemporary approach. The vivid blue is a color much loved by early Americans.

46

brick red and lamp black. Scenic murals, derived from copying French wallpaper and from the local countryside, were popular, and stencils were often used to facilitate the painting.

The background paint was simple whitewash, colored white, biscuit, pink, yellow, gray, light green or light blue. The furniture was sometimes painted in the greenish-blue color which we particularly associate with Sweden. The painters used a lot of cheerful red in their decorations, and window and door frames were sometimes painted in a contrasting color, a feature still common in America. Carpet was too expensive, and painters often made the best of the plain wooden floors by simulating mosaic tiles in squares and diamonds or by designing elaborate stenciled borders. Plain painted floors were also popular. Thick canvas floor cloths, painted with geometric designs, were another feature of this style.

It is easy to recreate the traditional look by painting and stenciling on walls and floors (see pp. 56, 180 and 181). If you decide not to paint the floors, plain polished wood or some matting will create the right warm but neutral

FIREPLACES BY ROBERT YOUNG

TOP: Here, a primitive scene extends across the whole width of the fireplace. The landscape with trees and houses is painted without any perspective. The pink sides of the fireplace have been distressed to give a slight mottled appearance.

BOTTOM: This fireplace is suitable for young and old alike. The sides of the fireplace have been mottled with a paint-filled brush which has been dabbed on to a slightly paler base. The central section is painted with a classic primitive scene including a farm house, a wooden fence, trees and animals. The decoy ducks on the mantelpiece are typical of American country interiors.

background coloring for an attractive looped or rag rug or perhaps an American Indian rug. Rag and looped rugs can be bought, but they are also simple to make yourself if you have the time. Rag rugs are also a feature of early Scandinavian and English homes, but braided rag rugs are distinctively American. A figurative rug, perhaps depicting an animal or a bird, can look charming hung on a nursery wall.

The Colonial settlers initially used a lot of oak as they had in England. They soon switched to the native maple, cherry and pine, however, and much solid country furniture is made in these three woods. The furniture tended to be simply made, in plain polished wood, but where good materials were scarce, early craftsmen often painted their furniture. The paint frequently concealed low quality wood or a mixture of woods. Stenciled cabinets, blanket boxes (which make excellent toy chests) and chests of drawers were common, and the designs were often very exciting and elaborate.

Nineteenth-century America was very much a society on the move, so furniture which was easily transportable had extra importance. Now that these simple styles are

TOP AND BOTTOM: This child's bedroom has recently been stenciled in an American Colonial style. The artist studied old American stencil designs and, rather than slavishly copying them, designed her own in the same style to fit in with the architectural elements in the room. Mantelpieces were often elaborately stenciled, and here the designer has used a formal swag to run across the cornice. Around the mantelpiece runs a ribbon of leaves with small birds at each corner. The baskets of flowers on the mantelpiece are very traditional. The artist used spray paint for the stencils with great precision. Less experienced artists would be better advised to use a brush with a small amount of acrylic paint.

A magnificent lion dominates this American hand-hooked rag rug, which was made in the second half of the nineteenth century.

popular again a lot of reproduction country furniture is being made, but you can also buy cheap secondhand wooden furniture, paint it in the moss green, terracotta red, slate blue and soft yellows that were so popular, and then perhaps add some stencils (see p. 172). An American Country cradle should either be in painted or natural wicker or be the popular rocking sort in old pine, which again can be painted. A trundle bed would make an ideal small bed as the child gets older.

On the bed should be the object for which America has become famous all over the world: the patchwork or appliqué quilt. The tradition of patchwork quilts came particularly from northern England and Wales, and many of the same patterns, such as the common Flower Garden, Feathered Star, School House and One Patch, are still made on both sides of the Atlantic. Patchwork was an art form born out of necessity when material was scarce and scraps were valued, but in America, particu-

larly among the Pennsylvania Dutch communities, the Amish and the Shakers, it achieved new heights with brilliant combinations of quilting, patchwork and appliqué.

You can buy old quilts or make your own, culling ideas from one of the countless books which are published on American quilts. Album quilts are particularly American and are thrilling for children. They are made up of squares – generally twelve squares in the case of a crib quilt – each of which depicts a different appliquéd design such as birds, houses, animals and garlands of flowers. As crib-sized quilts are difficult to come by, try making one yourself. This way you can also personalize the quilt by appliquéing or embroidering the child's name. Stenciled quilts with charming designs of animals and birds on cotton or calico are another delightful tradition. You can easily do this today on plain cotton sheets, pillowcases and duvet covers.

Elaborate curtains are not a feature of American Country style. If you want curtains, simple ones in calico would be most appropriate, with perhaps a simple stencil border. More often than not, the windows of early American homes had no curtains, and people relied on shutters to keep out the light. In the southern states, plantation shutters were invaluable for keeping out the cold in winter, and allowing currents of cool air to circulate in the hot summers.

OPPOSITE: A beautiful example of an early American quilt. These are now expensive and difficult to obtain. A similar result can be attained by using a stencil technique. Stencil the same border all around and then use four different square shaped traditional motifs in the center repeated to make up the appropriate number for your size of quilt.

51

Nowhere are Christmas rooms decorated with more care than in America. This room is dressed with stuffed cotton decorations including Santa Claus, a goose girl doll, animals, a dolls' house hanging, and a wreath, which are all available in kit form. On the bed is a splendid Christmas quilt.

In old American houses it is often the clutter that you remember, and this clutter looks particularly attractive in children's rooms. Wooden animals are very popular, particularly the decoy ducks which the first settlers copied from American Indians. Wooden dolls, animals and toys of all sorts make charming ornaments, as do wooden painted cut-outs of animals on the walls. Also on the walls hang primitive paintings, such as single portraits, family groups or animals, which are still being created today, as are samplers, which were also popular in Colonial times. You can make a sampler to commemorate your child's birth or to give to another child. Another charming toy is the patchwork animal, made at quilting parties.

Attractive baskets are a feature of early America, and these, particularly if lined with pretty cotton prints, are very useful for containing all the odds and ends your baby needs. The charming cottons with tiny designs which were used by the early quiltmakers are easily available both in America and in Europe, where they are sold in shops and by mail order (see Appendix). Also popular are American cutout cotton kits for making dolls, swans, Christmas wreaths, quilts and hangings. These feature in our Christmas room. They are a modern development of American Country style and none the less delightful for that.

This Christmas quilt is a combination of patchwork, appliqué and quilting. It was made entirely from American cottons printed in Christmas patterns of holly, mistletoe, etc. and measures 62 in (158 cm) by 80 in (199 cm). The twelve squares are 14 in (35 cm) across and include a traditional fir tree design in each corner, four different snowflake designs, a patchwork star, an appliqué partridge in a pear tree, an appliqué basket and, at the top, two appliqué turtle doves. These squares were all worked by hand, but the green and red strips which join them are machined, as is the red outside strip. Once joined together the quilt was tacked on to wadding, given a cotton backing and quilted. The edges are bound in red.

An illustration by W. W. Denslow for a 1903 edition of Denslow's Night Before Christmas.

PAINTING WITH STENCILS

The stenciled frieze in this nursery is based on a traditional early American design. The artist first planned her design on drawing paper, then traced it on to transparent paper and from there on to oiled manila paper. Experienced stencilers can create a wide range of designs and effects by making and cutting their own stencils. If you are a novice, however, it is advisable to practice with a pre-cut stencil pack before trying to cut your own. Many pre-cut stencils based on early American designs are now widely distributed in the USA and in Europe, and can be obtained from specialty craft stores and interior design shops.

The stencils in this illustration have been applied with spray paint. Remember that the fumes are quite toxic, and it should not be used with small children in the room or by pregnant women. If you are new to stenciling it is safest to use a stencil brush with acrylic or japan paints, or with specialty fast-drying stencil paints which minimize the danger of smudges.

The following instructions are for a two-color frieze like the one illustrated here.

MATERIALS
- 1 pre-cut stencil pack (this will contain two templates, one for each color)
- Pencil
- Masking tape
- 2 paint colors (use acrylic, japan or stencil paints)
- 2 medium stencil brushes
- Paint tray
- Step-ladder
- Paper toweling
- Turpentine

METHOD
1 Before you start, make sure that your wall surfaces are suitable for stencils. You can stencil on to emulsion and eggshell paint surfaces, but you cannot be assured of a good result if you stencil on to gloss paint.
2 Measure your stencil against the length of each wall. Start from the center and work outwards, making light pencil marks beneath the lower border of the template to act as a guideline when you start to stencil. If the design doesn't exactly fit the walls, "lengthen" it when you stencil by repeating a few details.
3 Secure the template for the first (dominant) color to the center of the first wall, using masking tape.
4 Pour a small amount of paint for the first color into the paint tray. Lightly dip one of your stencil brushes into the paint, then wipe off any excess on a piece of paper toweling. The less paint you have on the brush, the less risk there will be of smudges and smears.
5 Apply the paint by working across the template with light, even, circular strokes (see diagram i).
6 Repeat by gently lifting off the template and repositioning it so that the design continues uninterrupted; paint the next section.
7 Continue until you have completed the first color.

8 When the first color is completely dry, apply the second color using the second template and your second stencil brush. Follow the above method until the border is complete (see diagram ii).

9 After use, clean the stencil brushes and the backs of the templates with turpentine and wash them in warm, soapy water.

i

ii

iii

Chapter Five

ENGLISH COUNTRY STYLE

While very traditional, English Country is altogether different from the more classic Victorian style. In contrast to the sophistication and elegance of the latter, it evokes the world of the English country cottage in all its purity and simplicity, with old scrubbed pine tables and rocking chairs, rag rugs, curtains in muslin or gingham, and small windows through which gardens full of hollyhocks and sweet peas can be glimpsed. It is a style associated with the writings and paintings of Beatrix Potter, of Alison Uttley who with her illustrator Margaret Tempest gave us *Little Grey Rabbit*, and of Kenneth Grahame who created Toad and Mole and the unforgettable characters of *The Wind in the Willows*. In the world of these artists, friendly animals often inhabit cozy homes very similar to those of Edwardian cottagers. In its innocence, English Country is a style totally appropriate for children's rooms, especially rooms that are small or irregular in shape. There is nothing sophisticated or mass-produced about it. Everything is homemade, or at least looks as if it is. Country crafts are not just appreciated but are glorified.

If you live in an old house with uneven walls, low ceilings and beams, your child's nursery will be an ideal candidate for English Country style. You should probably resist patterned wallpaper and opt for emulsion or eggshell paint in clear warm shades of off-white, pink, yellow or perhaps a very soft green. You could also try sponging, ragging or color-washing, but not the more sophisticated technique of dragging. On these backgrounds you could add a frieze of stenciled flowers or animals, or use one of the many charming Peter Rabbit friezes that are available. If you want something more lively, pastel stripes or dots either on wallpaper or painted directly on to the emulsioned wall would look

Margaret Tempest's illustrations for Little Grey Rabbit *inspired the decoration of this room. The antique bedspread on the table is from the north of England. The curtains are made of old English patchwork. The chair and stool are oak, and on the wall is a Margaret Tempest alphabet poster.*

appropriate (see p. 164). Alternatively, you could consider a simple mural picture showing a country scene with animals, or perhaps a painted *trompe-l'œil* window with a cottage garden scene outside.

In the enchanting paintings of Margaret Tempest you will see the kind of curtains, tablecloths and quilts that are suitable for an English Country nursery. In *Little Grey Rabbit*'s world, curtains are made from checked gingham, calico or muslin; occasionally a simple floral print or spotted cotton is used. The curtains are short, hanging to just below the window; there is a frill along the top in the same fabric, but otherwise there is very little in the way of flounces and bows. Margaret Tempest's characters go to bed under voluminous quilts made of brightly colored patchwork. The colors are always soft primary colors or bright pastels such as sky blue and rose pink, lettuce green and daffodil yellow.

Eat Up Now! *by Margaret Tempest.*

Patchwork quilts are an old English tradition which was exported enormously successfully to America. Sometimes it is impossible to tell if a particular quilt comes from the north of England or the East Coast of America. Cottagers often used very basic square patches, but sometimes the quilts were infinitely elaborate. Colors could be very bright, and there was a strong use of red, which often originated in women's red petticoats. Country needlewomen also practiced intricate quilting on one-colour fabrics.

It is still quite easy to find old quilts, but they are expensive, rather delicate and rarely of crib size. If you have the time it is fun to make them yourself, using the many lovely floral prints available. Patchwork also looks lovely when used as a tablecloth reaching to the floor on a circular table, though you will need a large mat or perhaps a linen tablecloth on top to stop it from getting grubby. Curtains made in basic patchwork squares can look wonderful.

For sheer practicality you will probably choose to carpet the nursery, in which case opt for soft, plain colors. Ideally, though, you should have scrubbed wooden boards, not too highly polished, with pretty rugs – rag rugs, for example, are now coming into fashion again. Matting provides a good alternative to carpet, and with its soft brown coloring looks more cottagey and sets off rugs very well.

For the furniture, look for solidly made wooden tables and chairs in traditional country styles, made of old unvarnished wood such as pine or oak, or painted. Really chunky old pine pieces can look marvelous, and you can cheer up the most unpromising piece of cheap furniture with a lick of bright paint, perhaps adding a pretty floral motif. Margaret Tempest's animal characters relax beside the fire in pine rocking chairs or on upholstered

This child's room uses many elements typical of English Country style: the soft colors in pinks, blues and yellows, the floral curtains, the old pine bed with a simple patchwork bedspread, samplers on plain pink walls and much wickerwork. There are many characters in the room that come from traditional literature (for example, Peter Rabbit and his friends).

furniture loosely covered in floral cottons. Find pretty cushions in patchwork, needlepoint or knitting. Over a chair you could fling a traditional, multicolored crochet rug, a feature of many poor cottages.

If the room has a traditional fireplace, try placing a hardboard cut-out in front of it. Have a good-sized pine table for toys and clutter. Chests of drawers and cabinets can either be in plain scrubbed wood or painted a dull white; in either case you could add a painted or stenciled motif, or perhaps a flower or animal design.

LEFT: A goose-girl figure cut out of plywood. To paint a cut-out like this requires a certain amount of skill. The car, duck and bus shapes can be bought at children's stores and painted in cheerful primary colors. RIGHT: A feature of eighteenth-century households was the cut-out companion figure. Nowadays the subjects vary from fireside cats to baskets of flowers.

OPPOSITE: With its striking roof beams and apricot color scheme, rag rug and assortment of mobiles, this nursery has a very English Country character. French windows lead out to a garden, making this a perfect room for spring and summer months, when toys can easily be taken outside.

Your cradle will be an old willow cradle of the kind used by villagers for centuries, left in its natural basket color or painted white, or a wooden one, perhaps on rockers. The crib should be either painted or left in unvarnished wood. A bed with a pine headboard could take its place when your child moves out of his crib. Simple canopy or four poster beds featured in Margaret Tempest's illustrations – children love four posters, particularly if they can close the curtains right around. Make the bed up with sheets and blankets and an eiderdown rather than the more continental duvet.

Somewhere on the walls you should have some stitchery in the form of a sampler, or amusing animal scenes in plain wooden frames. You could also hang up pretty plates, either old or new (well out of the reach of children), and have some pieces of old china on the mantelpiece alongside the charming china representations of animals which are on sale everywhere. Try to find as much of the clutter of the countryside as possible, including items like corn dollies and hollowed out Hallowe'en pumpkins. English Country toys are quite simple ones like rag dolls, hobby-horses and knitted dolls and animals. If you work at it, this room will be the most welcoming and cozy-looking in the house.

These contemporary samplers are embroidered in traditional styles on coarse linen. You can easily design them yourself or buy them in kit form. They are framed in bird's eye maple, which is most striking, but a more rustic pine would be equally appropriate.

63

MAKING A CARDBOARD CUT-OUT

Cut-outs can stand in front of a fireplace, hang on the wall or sit on a mantelpiece or bookshelf. Contemporary cut-outs have evolved from the popular eighteenth-century companion pieces. These were nearly life-sized cut-out figures of friends or servants which stood in the sitting-room to welcome guests and give the house a lived-in feeling.

Cut-outs can be made of plywood or thick cardboard, depending on their size and where you want to place them. Painting simple cardboard cut-outs is a project which young children can easily be involved in. In the illustration the goose-girl is made of thin plywood and has been cut out with specialist machinery and painted. To make a more simple cut-out of cardboard, like the bus and duck illustrated here, you will need pre-cut templates.

MATERIALS

Option A
– Cut-out cardboard template (templates are sold in many toy shops)

Option B
– Thick cardboard
– Graph paper
– Tracing paper
– Pencil

Both options
– Craft knife
– Scissors

– Poster paint
– 1 in/2½ cm paint brush
– Fine paintbrush for details
– String
– Masking tape

METHOD

Option A
If you buy a ready-cut template, no preparatory work is necessary before you start painting. Many toy shops sell groups of plain cardboard templates such as zoo and farm animals, car and train sets.

Option B
1 First plan your cut-outs on graph paper, keeping the outlines as simple as possible. When you are satisfied with the shape and size of your design, transfer it on to a sheet of tracing paper.
2 Lay the tracing paper over your cardboard and secure the edges with masking tape. Cut around the outline with a sharp craft knife.

Both options
1 First, paint the background color of your cut-out and leave it to dry. Simple shapes can look very attractive in single colors, but if you want to be more adventurous, use additional colors and a fine paintbrush to add details like the doors and windows of a house, the wheels of a train, etc. You can add more imaginative decorations, such as flowers and doodles, if you like.
2 When the paint is dry, make tabs for hanging the cut-out using two pieces of masking tape and a short length of string (see diagram i). If you want to stand the cut-out on a piece of furniture, make a

support for it with a triangular piece of card measuring approximately one-third the height of the cut-out. First cut a right-angled triangle with a craft knife, then trim one side of the right-angle by a few degrees (see diagram ii) so that the cut-out will stand at a slight angle. Use two lengths of masking tape to secure the triangular support to the back of the cut-out (see diagram iii).

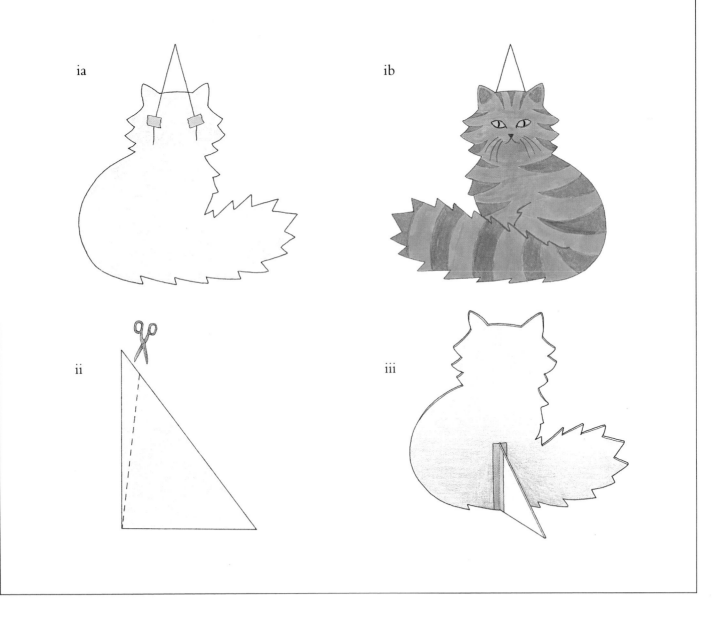

ia

ib

ii

iii

Chapter Six

SCANDINAVIAN COUNTRY STYLE

When we think of Scandinavian Country style, we think of wood-framed buildings with wood-paneled rooms. We think of brightly painted woodwork with painted and stenciled decoration, huge stoves, lively woven and embroidered tablecloths and rugs, and an overall feeling of warmth and comfort. With its simplicity and gaiety it is a style that really suits a child's room.

This tradition is not unique to Scandinavia. The use of wood and lots of painted furniture and decoration has a long history in Germany and Switzerland, with their wood-lined rooms, charming painted ornaments, cuckoo clocks and wooden carving. It harks back to a strong northern European peasant craft culture.

But Scandinavian countries developed a style of their own, which they exported to America and have carried on in more sophisticated ways to the present day. Nineteenth-century Scandinavians were farmers, living in isolated communities where long winters cut them off from the outside world. So naturally they made almost everything they used themselves. They built their own sturdy wooden houses, they wove their own rugs and bedspreads, and they embroidered cloths in lively Norse designs. Traveling carpenters would make solid furniture which was often carved with vivid decorations that had been passed down from Viking times. (The Swedish rococo style, evident in carving and embroidery and characterized by loops and swirls, may have been inspired by English embroidery of the seventeenth and eighteenth centuries.) The furniture was often a blue-green, or sometimes terracotta or yellow. There was a tradition of itinerant painters who would go from house to house with their stencils and paints, decorating rooms. Special rooms were set aside for celebrations, and these would be the most elaborately decorated.

Having studied Larsson's house, we added high shelves around the bed area of this room, and painted the walls a blue-green eggshell with terracotta details, and a biscuit color which was a favorite of Larsson's. Elaine Green, then created some delightful stencils based on Larsson motifs.

This charming stencil was inspired by a Larsson painting, Name Day at the Storage Shed, *but had Alice's initial incorporated along with bows which echo the daisy swags. It was stenciled with spray paint.*

Scandinavian Country is a style made accessible to us in particular by the Swedish artist Carl Larsson (1853–1919), who studied and worked in Paris from 1877 and was one of a group of Swedish artists who, in parallel with the French Impressionists, were preoccupied with man's relationship to nature and went out to paint in the countryside outside Paris. Larsson's French watercolors are wonderfully fresh and airy. But in 1885 he wrote, "Why in the name of all that's blue-green not paint

Simple calico curtains are typical of the Swedish style. Here they have been stenciled with an embroidery design taken from old Swedish embroidery. The stenciled daisy swags and the swag incorporating the child's initials were inspired by Larsson.

Swedish nature in Sweden itself?!" And he returned to Sweden with his wife Karin and their baby daughter Suzanne.

Once back in his home country, Larsson developed a real mission to reform the taste of his contemporaries by revealing to them the richness of Swedish peasant culture with its exciting carving and embroidery. He and other Swedish designers were strongly influenced by the work of William Morris and the Arts and Crafts movement in England, which reacted against the mass production and drabness produced by the Industrial Revolution. Larsson celebrated Swedish native culture both in his many marvelous paintings and, more importantly for us, in his delightful country house in Sundborn village. This house is now the most famous in Sweden.

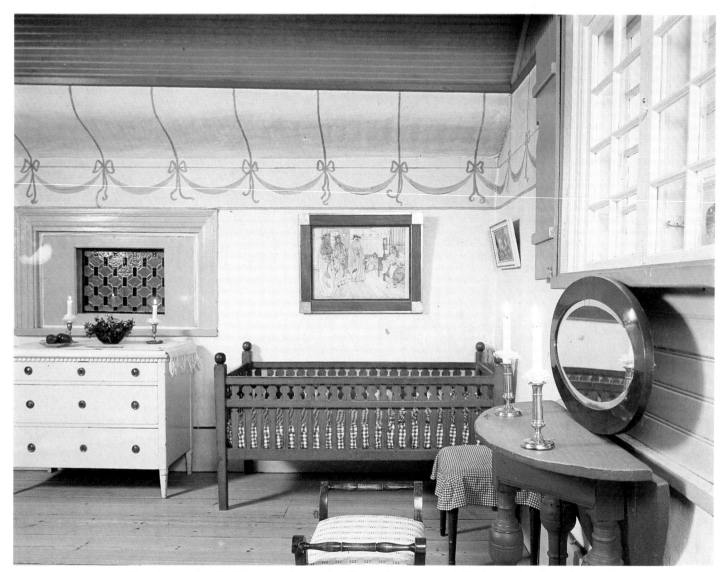

Karin's room in Carl Larsson's house, Sundborn, Sweden, in which Larsson's wife and two of their children used to sleep. The house, now a museum, was decorated throughout by the Larssons with great inventiveness and panache, as exemplified by the bows and swags motif used here. The child's bed, above which hangs a Larsson painting, was, at Karin's suggestion, made of pine chip, normally used as a roof covering material. The window to the left (facing east) was made smaller and set with colored glass in order to prevent the Nordic morning sun from shining in too brightly on the children.

Larsson's family home at Sundborn began as a small cottage. As he and his growing family spent more and more time there it was enlarged to become a sizable home, but it retained the feeling of intimacy you associate with a cottage. The house, looking very much the same, can still be visited, and books have been published about it. But you can also learn a lot about it from Larsson's own watercolors showing himself and his family in these enchanting rooms.

Most of the rooms are wood-paneled, and the wood is mostly painted. A limited range of colors is used, influenced by traditional Swedish interiors. While bright, they are also subtle and warm. The famous blue-green is particularly striking when contrasted with the rich terracotta of shelves and furniture. The rooms often have a plain colored wall (often a soft biscuit color) with painted friezes, using traditional Swedish patterns of trees and flowers or a painted edging, frequently in green. The decorative painting is very free and wonderfully attractive.

Larsson made a great feature of doors and windows, often surrounding them with a painted border or, in the fashion of the time, writing wise sayings or proverbs above the lintel. On the back of one door he made a delightful painting of his daughter Brita. He also personalized some of the rooms, writing the names or initials of members of his family above the bed or the door. Throughout the house he used carpets, runners and tablecloths embroidered in the traditional patterns of Swedish peasantry. The furniture is all solidly built but very stylish. The children's rooms are particularly enchanting with their green cribs and lovely wall paintings, and it was looking at these that persuaded us to decorate a child's bedroom in the Carl Larsson style (see p. 70).

Lisbeth with a Yellow Tulip, *a watercolor by Carl Larsson. N...* *the stencil on the wall with the child's initial, and the painted* *furniture.*

If you wish to do this, think first of your color scheme. The obvious background colors are a soft biscuit color, the somewhat muddy blue-green, a gentle terra-cotta, a soft warm yellow or a cool slate blue. If your walls and ceilings are of wood, so much the better. The green and terra-cotta look well together, as do the yellow and blue. Use a matte finish paint on the walls. Where the walls and ceiling meet, paint a band in a contrasting color. You could paint motifs around the doors and windows, perhaps using your child's initials, and you could apply a stenciled or painted frieze around the room or create a larger stencil on one wall. On the door itself, define the panels with a thin contrasting line of paint and try hand-painting or stenciling on the panels.

On the floor you should have either carpet or matting in a neutral color, or painted or varnished natural wood. The latter is not so practical for a baby, and you will need to add a large rug. Old Scandinavian rugs are almost invariably striped and are woven of wool or rags in shades of blue and white, red and white and sometimes yellow and red.

The stencil motif used on the walls can also be echoed in the furniture (see p. 172), which should be either natural scrubbed pine or painted in the greens, reds and blues which were popular in Sweden. Find either a natural willow cradle or a wooden one which could be painted. Then move on to a painted crib. A great feature of country beds in Sweden was that they were often built in against the wall. This made them particularly snug and looks very attractive.

Scandinavian curtains are never elaborate – they tend to be of calico, cotton or lace, sometimes with a simple, embroidered border, sometimes narrow stripes. Stencils can be used on bedspreads to brilliant effect.

In Sweden today many children's rooms are painted in styles that hark back to Larsson and the craft tradition that he revived. We hope that the delightfully airy but cozy room we managed to create for Alice will give you some ideas. Once you have mastered stenciling, the actual creation of such a room need not be at all costly. The most unappealing piece of old furniture can look stylish when given a lick of paint in one of the delicious colors from the Larsson palette.

Swedish child's room. This child's room in a 200-year-old Swedish country house at Odenslunda, near Stockholm, has been restored to its early charm, retaining the patina of age and leaving the painted walls as they originally were. The floor is simple pine. The frieze high up on the wall has been painted, copying an old one. The ceramic stove in the corner is a traditional feature of Scandinavian homes.

Brightly painted woodwork is a traditional feature of Scandinavian country homes. If you have doubts about your painting ability and want to practice on some small items, a good way to start is by painting some wooden toys for your child. Painted wooden toys also make amusing Christmas tree decorations.

Wooden cut-out animals can be bought in some toy shops and are often on sale in street market stalls, at craft fairs and at country shows. Or you might find second-hand ones at jumble sales, or in junk shops.

MATERIALS
- Wooden cut-outs or toys (see above)
- Paint: The type of paint you use depends on the effect you wish to achieve:
    GOUACHE or POSTER PAINT dries quickly, is easy to use and gives a flat effect. It must be painted with matte varnish to retain a flat look.
    OIL PAINT takes up to two days to dry but gives a more textured result and need not be varnished.
    ENAMEL PAINT creates a bright, shiny surface. It is more difficult to paint with but needs no varnish.
  Whatever paint you choose, make quite sure it is not toxic.
- Paintbrushes: Have a separate brush for each paint color. Select fine brushes appropriate to the type of paint you are going to use.
- Non-toxic polyurethane gloss varnish ⎫
- Small varnish brush   ⎬ Only necessary for gouache or poster paint
                                          ⎭

METHOD
1 Make sure the wooden toys are clean and free from dust before you start.
2 Decide whether you want simply to paint details on to the plain wood, or to paint the toys an overall base color before adding any details. If you take the latter option, apply two coats of paint of the color of your choice to each toy, allowing time for the paint to dry between applications. You need apply only one coat if you use enamel paint. Leave to dry.
3 Paint on details and decorations in the colors of your choice. For inspiration, you might look at needlepoint designs or fairground paintwork. If you are not feeling very adventurous, follow a simple color scheme of two or three colors using spots, stripes and zigzags. If you are painting toy animals, another option is to make them look more realistic, with stripes for tigers, spots for leopards, and so on.
4 If you are working with gouache, apply several coats of varnish, allowing time for each coat to dry between applications.

Chapter Seven

FRENCH STYLE

For centuries France, and in particular Paris, has been looked to for the latest in what is fashionable and chic, and this applies not only to clothes but also to furniture and room decorations. When an eighteenth-century Englishwoman described another's bedroom as looking pretty and "very French," this was a great compliment. For while the English, obviously with notable exceptions, have tended to muddle through, using furniture passed down to them in the family, the French have always placed much greater stress on smartness and on everything co-ordinating. This applies today even in children's rooms.

You have only to look at the catalogs of specialists in baby layettes, such as Descamps or Pierre Frey, to see that they have a look that is uniquely French. With their co-ordinated color schemes and smart finishes, they are extremely chic while remaining very charming and suited to children. The French pay considerable attention to their children's rooms as well as to their clothes, and always decorate a baby's room before he arrives. They are quite conformist, and as far as color is concerned they will go for rather simple statements to achieve an effect where everything must match.

If you wish to decorate a nursery in French style, first decide on your color scheme. To achieve the right effect, you must not deviate from the scheme you have chosen. The French often use pastel shades, without these being over-sweet or wishy-washy, and they also use a great deal of white which, while impractical, gives a very clean look. A cool blue is very popular, generally combined with white, but might not suit a north-facing room because it would appear too cold. Strawberry pink is often combined with turquoise, sky blue or peppermint green. Primrose yellow is also popular, and is frequently

One wall of this room has been carefully designed to provide storage space for all of a baby's requirements. This can later be used for the child's wardrobe and ever increasing toy collection. The yellow and lavender color scheme is highlighted by the frieze of farmyard animals.

matched up either with blue or with soft green. But the colors are not always pastel – you can use strong primary colors, particularly in a baby boy's room or in the rooms of older children. Here again, the combinations of colors must be limited. Red and white or perhaps red, white and blue look striking. So would a combination of vivid green and yellow.

Once you have selected the color scheme, think about the walls. French designers create splendid wallpapers, and companies such as Inaltera and Venelia produce delightful children's lines. These include modern as well as more traditional patterns. Among the latter are those

All the pastel colors in this modern nursery are brought together in the rainbow-striped curtains.

The soft blue, green and pink of this nursery form a co-ordinated color scheme that is repeated in the carpet and rug and the flowers on the wall. The floor cushions have a simple bold design, and the low cubes of foam rubber covered with fabric appliquéd with numbers are made to look like huge dice.

based on the famous French Toile de Jouy, which is very gentle and suited to children. Most of these wallpapers have fabrics to match, for making up into curtains, bedspreads and so on. The French are fond of putting fabric on their walls. This may seem strangely impractical in a child's room, but it is sometimes done and can of course look charmingly feminine.

You might opt for painted walls or for plain-colored wallpaper with borders, always keeping to your basic colours. In a more contemporary room you might try a blue "sky" background with simple white cloud shapes. Whatever you do, it should look very clean and finished.

This rule also applies to the furniture. The natural look is not appropriate for French style. Furniture should be painted with a matte finish, generally in white or in a color that co-ordinates with your overall color scheme. Painted wickerwork is popular, and for a baby's room a painted wickerwork cradle and matching chair would be just the thing. On the crib, chest of drawers, closet and table you might paint small motifs taken from the wallpaper.

In a more traditional bedroom, use curtains that match the walls. In simpler, more modern rooms, blinds are often used. Painted shutters are a feature of nurseries and indeed of all rooms in many older French houses. On the floor use an unpatterned, wall-to-wall carpet in either a co-ordinating color like light blue or a neutral biscuit or beige color.

Very good fabrics for crib covers and cushions are a crisp white piqué and of course the famous French eyelet, which decks the cradles of children throughout the world. Eyelet, either as material or as edging, is enchanting, and it combines well with many fabrics. It looks particularly charming with gingham on a child's patchwork crib quilt. Gingham is a material which is used a

Embroidered names and monograms are a hallmark of the French style. The cushion illustrated here shows an appliquéd doll holding a balloon which is embroidered with the name Marie. The pillowcase has a combination of appliqué and embroidery, and even the underpants are embroidered with a child's name.

great deal in France, as are other small checks. Many crib quilts are embroidered, perhaps with the baby's name or the alphabet or monogrammed initials, or they are appliquéd with a simple design. Ribbonwork, using pastel-colored satin ribbons on cushions or crib covers, looks very French and quite delightful. Ribbons are used a lot for piping and edging, which gives a chic look.

In total contrast to this rather sophisticated look, we cannot leave France without mentioning Provençal prints. These come in the most vibrant selection of colors and designs – buttercup yellow, scarlet, blue and deep mossy green – as well as some very subtle ones, and are ideal for children's clothes and rooms. This is a much more rural look. Provençal fabrics look well combined with natural wood or the natural wicker of babies' cradles or bassinets. They are exported a good deal – for suppliers, see Appendix. A baby's room entirely done up *à la provençale*, with frilled curtains and cradle, beautiful tablecloth and cushions and of course masses of baskets and dried flowers, would be very exciting indeed. A cautionary note: true Provençal fabrics often fade easily with much washing.

LEFT: This charming rose-colored set of pillow case, quilt, towels and sheets with appliquéd teddy-bears was designed for Descamps, the French firm whose style typifies the chic, co-ordinated look.

OPPOSITE: Children's bedroom by Pierre Frey. This room illustrates the very co-ordinated French style, with its color scheme of sugar pink, sky blue and peppermint green. The wallpaper design co-ordinates with the fabric on the beds. The wooden floor is painted in a cool blue which echoes the blue in the bedcovers.

FRENCH
STYLE

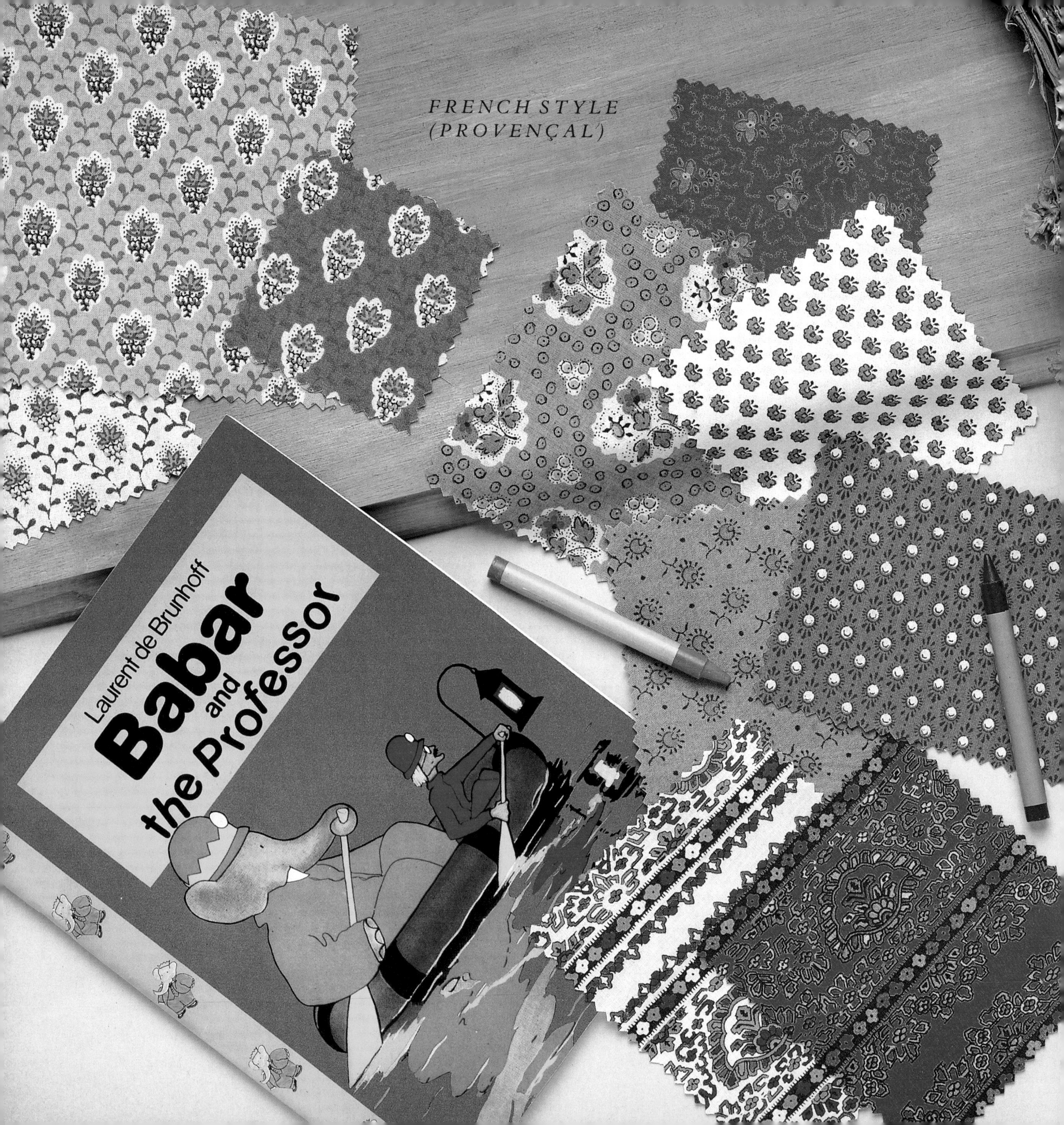
FRENCH STYLE
(PROVENÇAL)
Laurent de Brunhoff
Babar
and
the Professor

MAKING A BATH TOWEL WITH HOOD

Tiny babies have no strength in their necks. So a towel with a small hood over one corner can be very handy. Towels with hoods are also popular with toddlers, who enjoy playing "peek-a-boo" with the hood. The towel illustrated here is very much for bath-time use, but if you make one out of bright toweling fabric for expeditions to the beach, your children will enjoy adapting it as a hooded cloak for imaginary games.

MATERIALS (to make a towel 36 in/90 cm square)
- 1½ yd/1¼ m of toweling 36 in/90 cm wide
  4¾ yd/4⅓ m of bias binding approximately 1½ in/ 4 cm wide
  or 1 yd/90 cm cotton 36 in/90 cm wide (to cut into diagonal strips in place of bias binding)
- Scissors
- Thread
- Pins
- Needles

MAKING UP

1 Cut a square of toweling, each side measuring 36 in/90 cm. An easy way of doing this is to mark 36 in/90 cm with chalk or a pin along one side of the fabric, then fold the fabric diagonally at this point, forming a triangle. Mark along the edge of the triangle, fold back the fabric and cut along the lines you have marked to make the square. (See diagram i.)

2 Follow the same steps to make a small square for the hood, with each side measuring 14 in/35 cm. Double this square over into a triangle and cut along the diagonal (see diagram ii).

3 It is a good idea to bind the diagonal edge of the hood before attaching it to the towel. Pin the bias binding about ⅝ in/1½ cm from the edge, the reverse side of the binding facing the hood and with the edge of the binding overlapping (see diagram iii). Machine together. Fold the binding over to enclose the raw edges and hem to the other side of the towel/hood (see diagram iv). (See (6) below for instructions for making your own binding.)

4 Place the hood over one corner of the main towel so that the right angles of both are aligned (see diagram v). Pin together and machine sew the edges of the towel and hood.

5 Sew bias binding around the edge of the whole towel, following the instructions in (3).

6 If you want to make your own binding, cut diagonal strips 1½ in/4 cm wide out of the length of cotton and pin/sew together sufficient lengths to form two strips, one to edge the main towel and the other to cover the diagonal edge of the hood. Follow the instructions for bias binding in (3) above, but pin the binding to the towel, right sides

together, so that it can be folded and pressed after sewing in order to enclose the raw edge. Fold the free edge of the binding inwards by ¼ in/½ cm and press before hemming to the opposite side of the towel, as with the ready-made binding. Alternatively, to imitate the ready-made binding, both edges of the binding can be pressed inwards before sewing and you can proceed exactly as in (3).

7 As a finishing touch, you may like to embroider or appliqué something on the hood, perhaps in the same fabric as the binding.

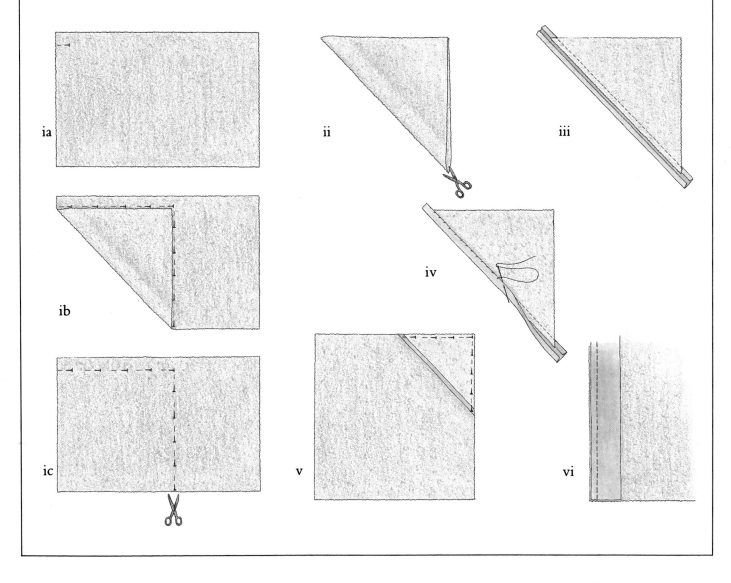

93

_____

THE NOW LOOK

If you revel in up-to-date design and clean, modern materials, such as steel, vinyl and plastic, the Now Look is for you. If you live in a modern house or apartment with large stainless steel windows and clear, clean lines, the chances are that many of the styles we have mentioned will be totally inappropriate for your baby's room and it would be silly to attempt them. The Now Look can be a riot of invention and fun, and is very appropriate for small nurseries in houses or apartments where space is at a premium. It is also much favored by small boys. There is no doubt that once boys are old enough to have a strong opinion, they make it clear that they don't go for frills. They want a much more jolly look. For this your house need not be modern. The room in the illustration opposite was done for a three-year-old boy in a nineteenth-century house, but it looks fine despite the gothic windows.

When you are deciding on your design you will find it helpful if you have one piece of modern furniture which sets the tone. Think also of a color scheme using clear primary colors, for a jumble of shades does not fit well with the clean lines of modern design. You might like to develop a theme – the theme in our picture (p. 95) was inspired by Alexander Calder's circus. Once that was decided, everything fell into place.

The work of modern artists can provide a good stepping-off point. It is, after all, in the work of abstract artists that we find many of the roots of modern design. Look at the paintings of Miró, Arp, Klee, the later Picasso, Mondrian or the later Matisse, all of whom at times drew wonderfully simple childlike creations, and ideas will begin to flow.

Wallpaper, unless it is very simple and geometrical, is not a good idea. As a background to the rather bold

This tunnel-like room has been divided into two separate spaces. A large blackboard gives character
to one wall. The decorator painted circus animals, jugglers and dancers on the curtains, duvet and
floor, and a free pattern of colored balls around the blackboard and window.

ABOVE: These curtains are made of ordinary sheeting material, lined with blackout fabric to make the room dark at nap time. The edges are bound with green bias binding so that the curtains stand out against the white wall. The paintings were done with special felt-tipped fabric paint pens and show circus artists.

OPPOSITE: This magnificent teddy circus quilt, designed and made by Cheryl Wade, measures 71 in (179 cm) × 56 in (142 cm). It is designed as a wall hanging and is a combination of quilting and appliqué. The embroidery, appliqué and quilting are done by hand, the rest by machine. The circus top squares are identical, whereas the six teddy squares show teddies in delightful circus antics from juggling to weight-lifting. The ringmaster squeaks if you press his tummy.

statements made by the furniture, pictures and hangings, it is far better to have a plain painted wall. This can be plain white, or a bright and clear but not too strident color, remembering that you want at all costs to keep the room light. The paint can be either matte or shiny. On the wall you might paint a blackboard or a very simple, stylized mural or frieze. Either leave the ceiling plain white or paint it in the same color as the walls, in which case you might paint a band or a simple frieze to define the top of the room. Or opt for a contrasting color.

Carpet is very comfortable for babies, but do choose a simple, clear color with little or no pattern or one of the more stylish, light-colored mattings. A bright cotton dhurrie will help ward off stains. Painted or stained wooden boards can look terrific but there is a high risk of splinters for a crawling baby, so cover them with a large rug for the time being. Vinyl-covered cork tiles are splinter-free, quite warm and easy to clean, and so is linoleum or cushioned vinyl. Later on you may wish to paint the floor (see p. 180–81), either with geometric patterns or with a road for little cars.

Curtains, if you use them, should be kept simple. They should be in a plain fabric or a large bold pattern or stripe, or they could be made of plain sheeting and painted. But this style really cries out for blinds. These come in a multitude of colors and can easily be painted. Modern Venetian blinds also look very elegant. For artificial light use spotlights, preferably the recessed, concealed variety which are rather expensive to install but have a terrific effect. You could paint a plain lampshade or use something bold and exciting like a kite instead.

Nowadays there is a lot of exciting cheap plastic furniture, as well as the high-tech furniture in steel and wire which is excellent for storage. Steel-framed wall racks and shelves can sometimes be bought from kitchen

suppliers and can be painted. Install a comfortable modern chair for yourself, and perhaps a bean-bag and some floor cushions. There are few interesting-looking modern cribs on the market, so opt for a plain painted one. When your child graduates to a bed, look for a simple design in painted tubular steel or make friends with your local carpenter and devise a bed in the shape of a car or a bus. Bunk beds are tempting, but don't buy them until your child is at least five and only then if there are no toddlers about.

The Now Look is a style which is very much reflected in the toys of the modern small child, like Duplo and Lego. It is also, in its use of modern materials and interesting shapes, ideal for mobiles, which make delightful presents and are a source of enormous fascination to a child from the first day his eyes begin to focus. You can make them out of a variety of brightly colored scraps of material – striped cottons or felt, for example, cutting out animals or star shapes or abstract triangles and squares. Cut out two of each shape, using templates or a paper pattern, sew the two together around the edges, leaving a hole at the bottom, then stuff with cotton wool and sew up. Some of the less obviously Christmassy Christmas decorations make excellent mobiles, and most of them already have hooks for hanging. You can make a wonderful mobile by just taking a wire clothes hanger, painting it and suspending objects from it.

For a central hanging, a simple mobile with three shapes using just one bar is easiest. This way you can get them to balance correctly. Once you introduce a second bar it is difficult to get the balance right unless your objects are all the same size and shape; the tiniest variance in weight makes a huge difference.

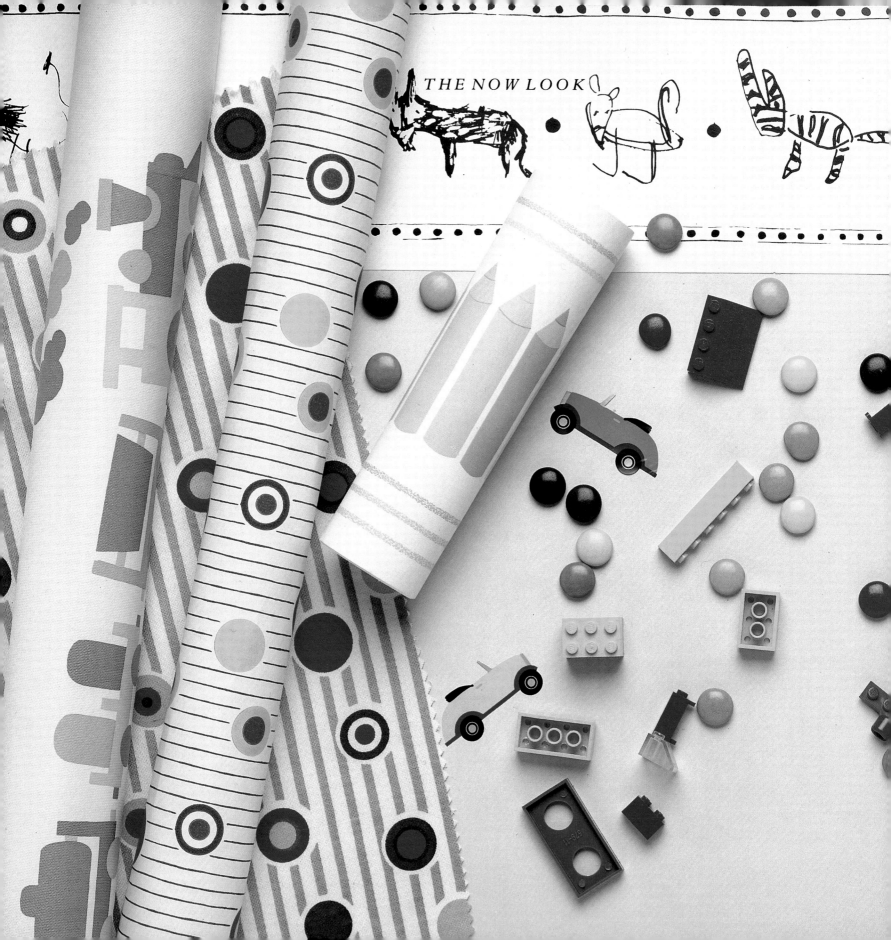

THE NOW LOOK

A blackboard is an invaluable addition to any nursery. It can be used again and again, and will provide hours of pleasure for small children and help them to develop their drawing skills. Blackboards painted directly on to walls are particularly useful in small nurseries, where a free-standing blackboard would take up valuable floor space. However, if you want a blackboard that can easily be removed at a later date, you may prefer to paint a piece of hardboard and then screw this on to the wall. The color need not be black. A dark color like deep green or midnight blue might suit a room better.

MATERIALS
- Sandpaper
- Black or dark paint: name brands of blackboard paint can be purchased at specialty art and craft stores. Alternatively, you can use eggshell paint, as in this example.
- 2–3 in/5–7 cm paintbrush
- Masking tape
- Scissors
- Pencil
- Graph paper
- Ruler

METHOD
1 First decide on the size and position of your blackboard. To do this, measure the wall upon which you plan to paint the blackboard and draw a thumbnail sketch of it to scale on a piece of graph paper. Include in your sketch any windows, doors and pieces of furniture that will stand against the wall. Remember that a large blackboard can easily overpower a very small room. Traditionally, blackboards are square or rectangular, but you may like to design one which is circular or half-moon-shaped.

2 Make sure the wall surface is in good condition. Use sandpaper to rub down any lumps and bumps. You can apply blackboard or eggshell paint to most paint surfaces, but not to woodchip paper or to old wallpaper.

3 Use a pencil and ruler to mark the outline of the blackboard on the wall.

4 Apply masking tape around the outer edge of the pencil line so that the blackboard has a clean border. Masking tape can stick to walls too well and can pull off old paint or paper when it is removed. To avoid this, remove excess stickiness by running your fingers along the tape, or use low-stick masking tape.

5 Apply the first coat of blackboard paint, working from the top downwards with regular strokes. Test a small piece of masking tape to make sure it is not sticking too well. If it is beginning to stick, remove it quickly before it dries and apply a new piece of masking tape. Leave the paint overnight to dry.

6 Apply the second coat and leave to dry.

7 Apply the final coat and leave to dry.

8 Carefully peel off the masking tape.

9 For a finishing touch, you might like to stencil a border around the blackboard, or frame it with a wallpaper border or a looser, painted zig-zag border. In the illustration, the area around the blackboard has been painted with balls and crosses, continuing the circus theme that characterizes the room.

Chapter Nine

MODERN ROMANTIC

This is a style which, while entirely contemporary, has nothing of the high-tech, minimalist look that we associate with much modern design. It is a very free style which contrives to transform a room into a magical environment through the use of pretty colors and shapes, murals, *trompe-l'œil* and visual jokes. The word romantic does not indicate lots of frills and lace. Everything about a Modern Romantic room is rather dreamlike and amusing, but it is a style every bit as suitable for boys as for girls. There is generally a theme to the room and often this will tell a story. The colors tend to be soft and delicate – sky blue, peppermint green, buttercup yellow and sugar pink – but remain clear and modern. It is an ideal style for a child's room.

On the walls you can use wallpaper in one of the many attractive and bold contemporary designs that are printed for children. These often have curtain material to match.

Spots and stripes can be fun, particularly if you paint them yourself (see p. 158). You can make a delightful spotty border or wall using the end of a cork dipped in paint to make your spots. And you can make friezes around the room and around the door and windows using potato prints. But the most exciting option is a mural.

While murals are a major feature of the Modern Romantic style, they need not be at all complicated. A tree made from sponging or potato prints, or a sprayed-on sky, are both extremely easy to create but can totally alter the mood of a room (see p. 163). The secret of a successful mural is to plan the theme and color scheme you want before you start.

If you are going to embark on a mural, decide whether you can make one yourself (see p. 166) or whether you will have to bring in an expert, which will not be cheap.

The main feature of this young girl's room is a large and imposing closet taking up the whole of one wall. The muralist designed an old-fashioned, fairytale house painted in muted colors as this would grow with the child. Some sky has been painted in to create depth and space.

Your theme might be nursery rhymes or songs, or it might be age-old children's stories like *The Three Little Pigs*, *Jack and the Beanstalk*, *Hansel and Gretel* or *Snow White*. All these narratives lend themselves to marvelous murals. Or you may prefer a charming country scene with flowers and animals, or a wispy sky with clouds and balloons floating past. The mural may spill over on to the ceiling. *Trompe-l'œil* windows are also a source of endless entertainment for small children.

If you choose to carpet the floor, use a clear, warm color which blends well with your color scheme for the walls. If you have chosen an outdoor theme then it would make sense to have the carpet grass-colored; if you have a naval theme, then choose a bright blue carpet. Witty contemporary rugs would look well. Alternatively, you could paint or stain the floorboards in a pretty color, perhaps decorating them with a pattern round the edge. Of course this would be less appropriate for the crawling years, when cushioned vinyl or gaily colored linoleum would certainly be more practical.

BELOW LEFT: This delightful playroom-cum-bedroom is a jumble of exciting features. The color scheme is clear and clean, and the primrose yellow walls provide a warm background for the collection of hats, toys and dolls.

BELOW RIGHT: Hey diddle diddle, the cat and the fiddle, an illustration by Jonathan Langley.

At the windows you might hang blinds. These can be in plain colors, with bold stripes or spots which you could paint yourself, or with a cheerful bold design or an illustration of balloons, animals, large flowers or even a *trompe-l'œil* window scene. Curtains have a very softening effect on a room, so they are quite appropriate for our romantic look. You can have plain curtains in a clear color, and perhaps edge them with a contrasting binding or paint designs on them with fabric paint. Or you can use a pretty patterned fabric. Frilled and ruched curtains look fine for this style.

The crib and other furniture should probably be painted either in white or in the strong, clear, almost innocent colors which are the hallmark of your room. The styles need not look modern. Old chairs when painted, perhaps with flower motifs and animals, suddenly take on a new and interesting life. On the other hand, chairs in surprising shapes such as animals are tremendous fun. You might make a four-poster or canopy bed for a little girl if she wishes, complete with all the frills. Painted baskets can be lined with lively modern cottons matching your baby's bassinet (see p. 20).

ABOVE RIGHT: Pretty pink fabric, billowy curtains and a canopy over the bed create a romantic mood for a little girl's bedroom. This canopy is a modern alternative to a four poster bed and is a good idea where space is limited. It can easily be assembled by attaching three rods to the wall and draping fabric over the rods.

RIGHT: The fresh and lively fabric contrasts well with the clean white walls of this bedroom. The co-ordinated look is achieved with matching fabric for the curtains and chest of drawers, and a contrasting headboard fabric that is repeated in the blind. The base board around the wall is bright red, in refreshing contrast to the white walls.

The two child-sized chairs in this illustration are extremely versatile and can be used indoors and out. They are collapsible, so they can also be put away and stored without taking up too much space. The mural was painted according to the method described on p. 166.

Built-in furniture suddenly takes on a new life if you transform a half- or full-length cabinet into a dolls' house or a house for imaginary games, or just break up the dull surface with simple motifs such as stars, balloons, bows or a flock of birds. If you want to create a bolder, *trompe-l'œil* effect, a single cabinet might become an archway or door leading into a secret garden.

If you keep the walls simple you can adorn them with hangings, either painted or appliquéd in cotton or other fabrics with interesting textures. The Advent calendar, (p. 112) is a perfect idea; as are pictures with nursery rhyme themes. Mobiles made of wood, painted paper cut-outs, papier mâché, or stuffed fabric shapes will add to the cheerful feel of this room. So will bean-bags, either in a sturdy patterned cotton or painted in designs that co-ordinate with the curtain fabric or the colors of your walls.

TOP LEFT: The cottage and shop in this attic nursery is a perfect place to develop a child's imaginative play from two onwards.

TOP RIGHT: Low cabinets for storage have here been transformed into a row of terrace houses. This is an excellent way of combining a play area with storage space in a small nursery.

BOTTOM RIGHT: Striped seaside huts have been machine-sewn in bright ice-cream colors on a crib quilt designed by Jenny Hutchison.

LEFT: To introduce an airy, Mediterranean character to a child's small room the artist has used a mixture of cool blues, aquamarines and gray-blues.

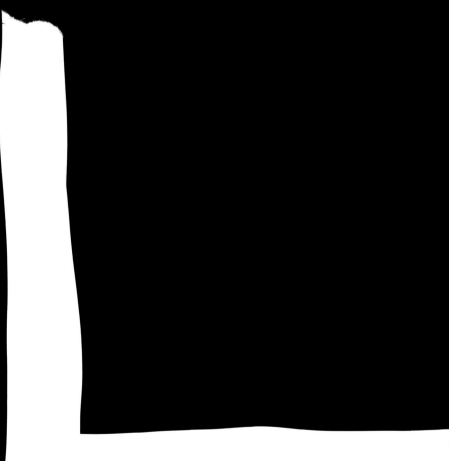

MAKING A "SURPRISE" ADVENT CALENDAR

This is an Advent calendar with a difference. It has been made with old scraps of fabric, and it can be hung on the wall and used year after year. There is a different pocket for each date. The odd numbers open to reveal appliqué pictures, while the even ones hide secret pockets for surprise presents.

MATERIALS
- 1 piece of plain cream cotton 36 in/90 cm square
- Lining: 1 piece of the same cotton 45 in/115 cm × 39 in/100 cm
- 12 cotton "pockets" 4 in/10 cm × 3½ in/9 cm, made from the same cotton
- Contrasting cotton for border:
    2 red strips approx 45 in/115 cm × 2 in/5 cm

1 red strip 36 in/90 cm × 2 in/5 cm
1 blue strip 36 in/90 cm × 6 in/15 cm
- 48 printed cotton pieces 4 in/10 cm × 3½ in/9 cm, to make both sides of 24 windows
- Scraps of cotton or ribbon for 24 button-hole loops and 2 loops for hanging the calendar
- 48 pretty buttons
- 12 pictures, e.g. picture patches as used for sewing on to children's clothes
- Numbers 1 to 24 and the lettering for "MERRY XMAS", cut out of different colored felt (or you can use printed fabric and oversew the edges)
- 12 small "presents", e.g. model animals, erasers, sweets, chocolate coins
- Needles, pins, scissors and thread
- Measuring tape/ruler

MAKING UP
1 To make the 24 button-hole loops, cut strips of fabric about 2 in/5 cm × 1 in/2½ cm, fold along the length of each strip (reverse sides together) and stitch together ¼ in/½ cm from the edge (see diagram i). Turn right sides out and press.

2 Stitch the felt numbers on to the right side of 24 of the window pieces. Pin a button-hole loop folded in half to the center of one long edge of each piece of cotton – to the right of each number, with the loop pointing inwards. Sew together ¼ in/½ cm from the edges of the loop and the window piece (see diagram ii).

3 To line the windows, pin them – right sides together – to the remaining 24 cotton pieces, and sew each together with a seam of ¼ in/½ cm, enclosing the button-hole loop and leaving a gap of ¾ in/ 2 cm along one edge (see diagram iii). Trim the corners, turn each pocket right side out, stitch the gap and press.

4 The calendar is divided into 36 squares each measuring 6 in/15 cm × 6 in/15 cm (see diagram iv). Mark these out either with lines of stitching, or with pins or dressmaker's chalk, though the last can leave a slight stain. Stitching along the left-hand side of each window, sew the 12 odd-numbered windows in random order to the calendar (as in diagram iv) and stitch a picture patch under each one.

5 Repeat with the 12 remaining even-numbered pictures, this time sewing a cotton pocket under each to hold the "presents." Pull out the thread used to divide the fabric into 36 squares.

6 Pockets: fold the edge of each piece of fabric and press into a hem of $\frac{1}{4}$ in/$\frac{1}{2}$ cm. Fold one of the short edges over again by $\frac{1}{4}$ in/$\frac{1}{2}$ cm, press, and hemstitch to the back of each pocket (see diagram v). Place each pocket under a window, the folded edges facing inwards and the stitched hem at the top to form the pocket opening. Sew on to the calendar along the three unstitched sides.

7 Sew on 2 buttons for each window (see illustration), one to keep it closed and the other to keep it open once the day has passed.

8 Border: sew the "MERRY XMAS" lettering to the blue strip of fabric and, following the instructions for button-hole loops, sew two loops (for hanging the calendar) to each top corner of the blue strip. Pin and machine-sew the red strips along three sides of the calendar and then attach the blue strip – see the illustration.

9 Lining: pin the lining cotton to the front of the calendar and sew together, enclosing the loops and leaving a gap of a few inches. Trim the corners, turn right side out, sew up the gap and press.

10 Fill the pockets of the even-numbered windows with presents, with a special one for window 24.

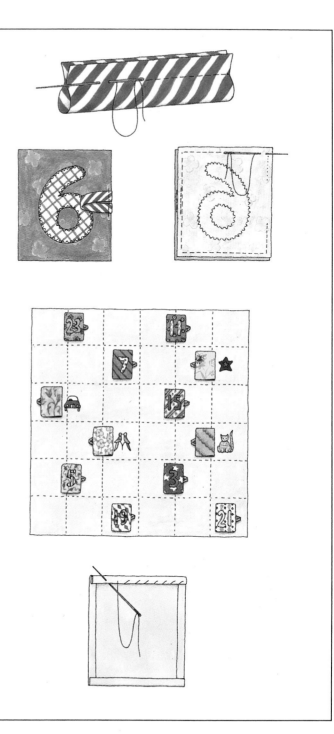

Chapter Ten

———————

EXOTIC

We live in a world where ordinary people travel infinitely farther and to more exotic places than their grandparents ever dreamed of. But it is not just people who travel – exotic goods do too. Even if you are not among the lucky ones who visit India, China, Thailand, Kenya or Peru and return laden with treasures, you can find the exciting handicrafts from these countries available in shops just down the street. Some of these goods are very sophisticated, some extremely basic, and often they are amazingly cheap particularly when one considers the amount of work involved. Their bright colors and simple styles make them enormously appealing to children.

So whether you have money to spare or are on a very tight budget, consider whether your child would enjoy having his bedroom decorated with the trappings of the East. Of course the room need not be entirely ethnic. Many Indian rugs, Chinese ornaments and Peruvian wall hangings look particularly striking when set against the stark, clean lines of a child's room decorated in very modern or high-tech style. But if space is a problem for you and you want to create a bright, inexpensive nursery for your child in a tiny cubby-hole of a room, the exotic look is an excellent option to follow.

The wall and floor surfaces of an exotic nursery can be prepared with minimum expense. The walls should be very plain, to set off the variety of brightly-colored fabrics and ornaments you are going to use. It does not matter if the walls are quite uneven; in fact this will give a more natural look. So will exposed beams. You could paint the walls in off-white or soft yellow tones – wallpaper is obviously out. On the floor fiber matting would look well, in a good neutral colour which will set off bright rugs. Alternatively, you could leave the wooden boards bare and lay rugs over them, making sure

The father of this little girl travels all over the world, so her nursery is an Aladdin's cave of
colorful treasures that he brings back from his travels. However, you don't need to globe-trot to
collect these items; many of them can be purchased in ethnic shops.

*LEFT: A very simple but regal playroom in the palace of an Indian maharajah at Deeg.
The padded carpet and floor cushions make for great comfort underfoot.
RIGHT: Midnight: Mother and Sleepy Child by Utamaro.*

the rugs are firmly secured. Alternatively, you could be very bold and stain the boards in a color that would marry with the colors of the rugs and bedspreads you plan – a moss green could look exciting, for instance, or vivid Chinese red. Cork tiles would also make an extremely practical floor.

For rugs and toys, visit the ethnic shops in your area. India and Pakistan produce stunning selections of rugs, and they often cost very little. The brightly-colored striped cotton dhurries from different parts of India are ideal. They are tough and you won't mind if they get messy in the rough and tumble of a child's bedroom. The most delightful nursery rugs are the soft white woolen Numdah rugs from Kashmir, embroidered in brightly-coloured wools with patterns of flowers and birds. The Kashmiris also make smaller rugs for children, with patterns like alphabets and snakes and ladders. Rugs from South America come in more earthy colors, in particular the lovely herbal-dyed Ayacucho rugs from Peru. The white Flokati rugs from Greece are lovely and warm for a nursery; they look like huge sheepskins and are wonderfully soft underfoot. They can be washed to keep their color and fluffy texture.

Instead of curtains at the windows you may choose to hang attractive blinds made in wicker or bamboo, though these may let in too much light. There are also

116

some lovely woven shades in bright colors from Colombia. Indian bedspreads make marvelous curtains, particularly those which show scenes of elephants and other animals. They are usually quite thin, so they should be lined. Cottons from Thailand and other parts of Asia are often brilliantly colored and of excellent quality, making them good for cushions, bean-bags and chair covers as well as for curtains. *Kikois* are lengths of cloth from East Africa, printed in brightly-colored bold patterns. They are quite thin, so, again, they must be lined, but they make most attractive bedspreads, curtains, tablecloths, cushions and bean-bags.

Your furniture should be quite plain, probably in scrubbed wood or bamboo. The cradle should be of basket work, lined with a soft Indian cotton. When the baby graduates to a bed you might find an exciting carved headboard or one of bamboo. On the floor lay bold floor cushions or bean-bags. In this ethnic setting life is conducted at floor level. When the child is a lot older you could hang up a brightly-colored Brazilian hammock. All the baby's paraphernalia, and later his toys, can be stored in reed or bamboo baskets.

For lighting use simple spotlights, or buy a charming umbrella from Thailand or China and adapt it for use as a lampshade. Cheap Chinese paper lanterns also make excellent overhead shades. There is a huge variety of

RIGHT: Chinese goods are sold everywhere nowadays, and you can often find the most enchanting objects to decorate a child's room at very little cost. Shown here are some charming cushions in a combination of quilting and appliqué, beside the traditional folding silk-covered waste paper basket which comes in all sizes and can be used for many purposes. The fan, embroidered slippers and variety of animal-shaped baskets make wonderful ornaments. On the wall are animal cut-outs and a cat mask.

Baby lambs and bright blue borders make this a perfect nursery mirror.

117

mobiles to buy. Mexican parrots made of papier mâché come in brilliant colors, while from Chile come copper birds. The Chinese make marvelous mobiles from paper, as well as kites that look like dragons.

On the walls you can really have fun. From India come marvelous paintings on cloth in exciting colors, showing mythical scenes which often involve animals. There are also mirrorwork hangings (mirrorwork is best left on walls with babies about, not used on cushions). Chinese scrolls can be very pretty, as can many Chinese paintings. There are Mexican bark paintings showing exotic birds, and woven cloths from Ecuador in animal shapes. Most exciting of all are the Peruvian patchwork banners. These are made of scraps of bright cotton and often show scenes from village life. Their particular charm lies in the fact that the little people and animals portrayed on them are made as separate dolls and then attached to the banner. This is really exciting for a small child, but it is important to keep the banner out of the reach of babies.

Simple ethnic toys make lovely ornaments. But make sure that babies and toddlers cannot reach them, as the paints may not conform to safety regulations and should not be chewed. Children are fascinated by exotic birds and there are lots to choose from. Everyone seems to make ducks. There are painted wooden ducks from Thailand and papier mâché ducks from Sri Lanka. The Chinese make marvelous tiny china ducks and they come in painted balsa wood from the Amazon. Later on a child may love to make a duck collection. Or he may make a collection of exotic shells or foreign dolls.

Not only is an exotic room fun to decorate, it is also a way of telling older children a bit more about the world they live in. For all their diversity, there is a lot that links the many cultures which have contributed to your child's magical room.

Colorful banners such as this are traditionally made in the villages of Peru and they show village, landscape and festival scenes. They are now easy to track down in Europe and America and they make delightful gifts. They might also give you ideas for a simple appliqué you could do yourself. The banners are made of many brightly colored cotton scraps appliquéd on to a sheet of cotton and stuffed to create a three-dimensional surface.

OPPOSITE: This treatment is the answer to a defunct bedroom fireplace. Its design reflects a strong Persian influence. The pillars are painted with bright yellow Assyrian lions and trees, while along the top are painted Eastern domes.

119

EXOTIC

MAKING AN AFRICAN BEAN-BAG

This very simple bean-bag was made from a *kikoi* from Tanzania. You could equally well use a *batik* from Indonesia, *longgi* fabric from Burma, or any bright cotton design that appeals to you. As most cottons from hot countries are quite thin, and as you will need to wash the bean-bag from time to time, it is sensible to line it with plain cotton and to sew double French seams to ensure that the polystyrene granules do not leak out.

MATERIALS
- 1 strip of cotton: sheets of fabric from exotic countries vary in size. You can adapt this pattern to suit the fabric you have, but for a good-sized bean-bag you will need a piece of material measuring 36 in/90 cm × 4 yd/3.5 m, or larger.
- 1 piece of plain cotton lining fabric the same size as the outer fabric.
- Polystyrene granules (2 large bags were used here, but the quantity depends entirely on the size of the fabric and how firm you want the bean-bag to be).
- 16 in/40 cm or 18 in/45 cm zipper (for outer fabric)
- 12 in/30 cm zipper (for lining)
- Pins
- Needles
- Thread
- Scissors

MAKING UP

1 Handwash the outer fabric in cool water, leave to dry, then iron out any creases. Don't be tempted to use hot water or a machine wash, as the dyes of ethnic fabrics are often prone to running in any but the coolest temperatures.

2 For the central section of the bean-bag, cut a strip of fabric $2\frac{1}{2}$ yd/2 m × 36 in/90 cm (these measurements can vary, according to the size of the design on the fabric). Pin the two shorter edges together to form a tube, and sew using a French seam. To make a French seam, first sew the fabric reverse sides together, stitching $\frac{1}{2}$ in/1 cm from the edge. Turn the fabric inside out (right sides together), iron flat and sew another seam, so that the raw edges are completely enclosed (see diagram i). Turn the fabric right side out and press the seam. Sew two parallel rows of gathering stitches along each open edge of the tube (see diagram ii).

3 For the top and base of the bean-bag, cut out two circles 20 in/55 cm in diameter. Fold the base circle in two and cut in half. Place the "outer" zipper centrally along one straight edge of one half section, marking where each end will lie (see diagram iii). Oversew the two cut edges before stitching the two halves together, leaving a gap for the zipper. Press open the seams and then sew in the zipper (see diagram iv).

4 Pull the gathering stitches on the top and bottom of the central "tube" section and pin to fit the two circles – reverse sides of fabric together if you wish to make French seams (see diagram v). Sew together, following the instructions for French seams given in (**2**) above, before turning right sides out via the open zipper. Press seams.

5 Follow the same steps for the lining. Place the completed lining inside the outer bag so that the zipper in the lining lies beneath the zipper in the outer fabric (see diagram vi). Fill the whole bean-bag with polystyrene granules and fasten the zipper in the lining. As a precaution against small prying fingers, turn the filled lining within the outer bag so that the inner zipper faces the bottom circle of the bean-bag and there is no danger of an inquisitive young toddler getting at and possibly devouring the granules. Finally, fasten the outer zipper. (The zippers are not wholly necessary, but they are useful because bean-bags need to be refilled periodically with granules in order to keep their shape. In addition, the outer bag can be removed more easily for washing.)

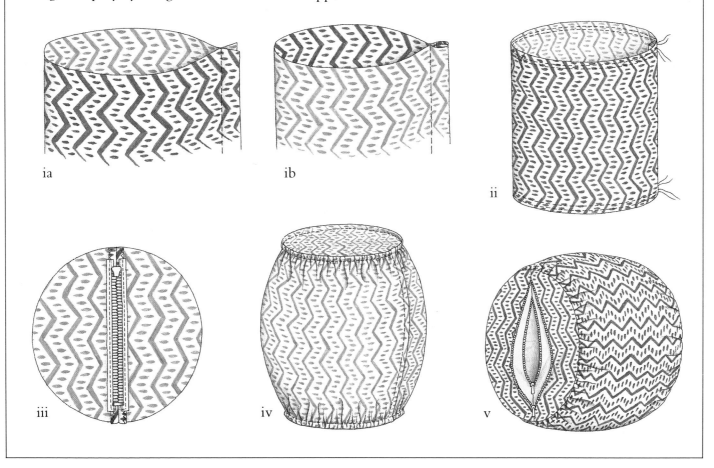

ia

ib

ii

iii

iv

v

A looking-glass with Alice and Humpty-Dumpty.

Part Three

————

NURSERY DETAILS

Chapter Eleven

CLASSIC NURSERY TOYS

The two toys which traditionally feature in nurseries are rocking horses and dolls' houses. The earliest dolls' houses were made in Germany in the sixteenth century – the first one we know of being made for Prince Albrecht of Bavaria in 1558 – and by the late seventeenth century they were quite common among rich families, though they were not regarded as toys for children. Germany later became a great toy-making center, and dolls' houses, and more particularly dolls' furniture, were exported throughout Europe and, more especially, to America during the eighteenth and nineteenth centuries. Dutch craftsmen also made exquisite dolls' houses, sometimes in the form of cabinets.

The craze spread to England, where they were called baby houses, and the earliest existing model is the late seventeenth-century Ann Sharp Baby House, in the form of a glass-fronted cabinet. It seems that English dolls' houses were made for children actually to play with, though this would plainly have been under supervision. The glass-fronted cabinets could easily be copied today; in furniture stores you can often find old cabinets which could do the job to perfection if painted and papered. The most dazzling eighteenth-century example is the dolls' house made by the estate carpenter at Nostell Priory around 1735, which has a majestic façade. Such precious toys were fitted with locks. A much later dolls' house in this grand tradition is Queen Mary's Dolls' House, designed in the early twentieth century by Sir Edwin Lutyens.

By the nineteenth century dolls' houses were commonplace in Europe and America, but with mass production the standards of production started to deteriorate. However, many exciting models survive which reflect changing fashions and styles.

Teddy bears were created at the beginning of this century,
and have dominated the nursery ever since. This splendid collection is seen having
a rather grand Teddy Bears' Picnic.

In America it is particularly difficult to identify the provenance of dolls' houses; many were imported, but they were also made by craftsmen recently arrived from Germany or Holland. By the mid nineteenth century the American toy industry was well established, and a particular feature of American dolls' houses is the use of tin and pewter both in the houses and the furniture. The delightful gingerbread houses produced by Bliss at the turn of this century were a great success when exported to Europe. American toymakers were also more modern than their European counterparts. Before the First World War there were dolls' houses with plumbing that produced water out of faucets, and the first houses fitted with electricity.

BELOW LEFT: The Ann Sharp Baby House, the oldest existing English dolls' house, made in the late seventeenth century in the form of a cabinet. It was given to Ann Sharp, one of the fourteen children of John Sharp, Archbishop of York, by her godmother Princess Ann.
BELOW RIGHT: This magnificent dolls' house at Nostell Priory was designed around 1735 and is said to be a copy of the design for Nostell itself. It is attributed to Colonel James Moyser, an amateur architect, and, the superb interior decoration was designed by James Paine.
OPPOSITE, TOP LEFT: This dolls' house comes from Beatrix Potter's house, Hill Top, at Sawrey, in the Lake District.
OPPOSITE, TOP RIGHT: A rare eighteenth-century English dolls' house from Bethnal Green Museum.
OPPOSITE, BELOW: The day nursery of the exquisite dolls' house built for Queen Mary by Sir Edwin Lutyens.

DAY NURSERY

The first rocking horse ever made is believed to have been the one given to Charles I, the ill-starred future King of England, when a boy in 1610. It was a pretty solid affair with rockers and a horse's head. Much later came the really beautiful carved horses on rockers, usually painted in dappled gray, which were in all nineteenth–century day nurseries. Sometimes these had the exciting addition of little seats at each end of the rockers on which other children could play seesaw. Later in that century we find the rather more stable invention of a horse whose feet are attached to two parallel bars mounted on a fixed platform. But today we just as often find rocking horses based on the original simple rocker design, and these give countless hours of pleasure.

OPPOSITE: A comparatively modern rocking horse, made from the pattern that was common from the latter half of the nineteenth century. It would make a handsome addition to any nursery.

BELOW: This ingenious rocking horse doubled as a kind of see-saw for the lucky children of Helen, Duchess of Albany. With the duchess are her children, Princess Alice and Charles Edward, Duke of Albany (in the kilt), and their cousins, Prince Alexander (left), Princess Victoria Eugenie (right), and Prince Leopold of Battenburg (baby). The photograph was taken in 1890.

132

The urge to collect is very strong in children from an early age. Making collections, whether of glass ornaments, cars, foreign dolls, shells or just pretty stones or bits of broken china, is particularly exciting to them. As they get older the rather rudimentary collections will become more elaborate, and nurseries should be equipped with shelves or cabinets to house these treasures in safety. Collections can be handed down from generation to generation, and if you collected something as a child, like the teddy bears and foreign dolls in our illustrations, house them prettily to delight your children.

Dolls in national costumes are easy to find wherever you travel and make exciting presents. Groups such as these merit prominent display.

Girl with a Doll's House, *by an anonymous artist. This very simple form of dolls' house, with three floors and a curtain across, was very common in the nineteenth century and can easily be made today either from scratch or by converting an old cabinet.*

133

─────────

Chapter Twelve

THE LINEN CLOSET

There is something so pure and innocent and beautiful about a tiny baby that one's instinct is to buy him the most exquisitely pure and beautiful things. This explains why many people spend a vast amount on a baby's first layette. However, there is no reason why these early first possessions should be too expensive if you make them yourself, and luckily many layette items are very easy to make. So in the period before the baby arrives and all the fuss begins, plan the baby's linen for the next year, from his bassinet to his crib, along with all the trimmings that go with them.

You are bound to need a lot of sheets. There will be regular accidents in the early days, and once the baby is teething he will soak the sheets with dribble. You don't want to spend your life panicking in case you run out of linen before the next wash. If you buy lengths of cotton flannel in white, blue or pink, you can make excellent sheets. Make them big enough to fit your baby's cradle as well as the bassinet.

Once your baby graduates to a crib you will need larger sheets. If you have some full-sized sheets which you don't use, perhaps because they are torn or unmatched, you can cut these up and make crib-size versions. With a little invention you can make something charming. Try edging the top sheet with a pretty band of cotton fabric, perhaps gingham or a small flower print, about 2–3 inches (5–7.5 cm) wide, and then edging it with eyelet. Make a pillowcase to match, perhaps with the baby's initials or a little flower or balloon appliquéd in one corner and eyelet around the edge. (Remember that a pillow for a tiny baby, if he uses one, should be very flat or he could suffocate.) Once he is in a crib your baby may use a thin duvet with a duvet cover, which is extremely easy to make. You can buy attractively printed sheeting

These co-ordinated French pillows, sheets and towels show just how pretty children's linen can be.
To achieve a French look care should be taken to choose only one or two colors and keep them close
in tone.

materials for babies, or just use pretty, percale cotton. More elaborate duvet covers, such as the dazzling circus one on p. 96, can later become wall hangings.

The baby will also need some towels. A towel with a hood over one corner is particularly helpful in those early weeks when his head is so wobbly, and it will keep him very snug. Hooded towels are easy and cheap to make (see p. 92) and can be charmingly personalized. An ordinary hand or bath towel can also be embroidered or appliquéd, and makes a simple but delightful gift.

QUILTS

The most noticeable item on a baby's crib is the quilt. Here it really is worth investing time, if not money, in something lovely. If the quilt is interesting enough, like many of the quilts we illustrate, it can be hung on the wall later. Whatever you decide to make, be sure that your scraps are in durable colorfast cotton which can stand up to regular washing. Quilts last better if they are hand-washed. You can make a simple patterned cotton quilt, lined with 2-oz wadding, with lace or a frill around the edge in the same or a contrasting fabric, or you can do some delicate embroidery or ribbonwork on the quilt, as is so popular in France. Some of the most exciting quilts are those in patchwork or appliqué or a combination of the two.

Patchwork quilts look delightful in children's cribs, whether they are the simple squared variety, which can easily be made on a sewing machine, or a much more complicated design. Americans boast the most marvelous appliqué quilts, and while your needlework may not be up to the standard we illustrate, you might try a much simpler version, perhaps with fruit and flowers or the shapes of rabbits, teddy bears and other

TOP: "Bow tie" and "teddy bear" fabric from Bundles in nursery shades of pink and blue.
ABOVE: A modern French fabric in unusual fresh colors from Descamps. The window motif could be used as a design for a mural.
OPPOSITE: "Ellaflumps" fabric from Bundles, co-ordinated with their grass wallpaper and garland, butterfly and "Ellaflumps" borders.

nursery animals. Once the patterns have been appliquéd on, make the quilt up and sew in tiny running stitch around the edges of the designs, piercing all the layers of wadding and the lining. To quilt successfully you must tack all three layers of the quilt firmly together to keep them in place as you sew.

Not many of the best quiltmakers working today bother to make crib quilts. This is largely because while people are willing to spend a small fortune on a quilt that will stay on an adult's bed for twenty years or more, they will not invest much in a child's quilt, which has a shorter working life. Deirdre Amsden is an exception. She is best known for her brilliantly sophisticated adult quilts, but

has done some enchanting and lively crib quilts using a mixture of patchwork and appliqué to brilliant effect. Jenny Hutchison's modern machine-made quilts are stunning. The patchwork elephant and the boats are both traditional patterns which gain a sharpness and modernity when done on a machine.

(a) and (b) These contemporary machine-sewn patchworked quilts measure 2 ft by 3 ft and are made in cotton. They are lined with polyester and hand-quilted.

(c), (d), (e) and (f) These highly original designs by Deirdre Amsden are works of art in their own right, and will make magnificent wall-hangings once they have completed their service as crib quilts.

c

d

a
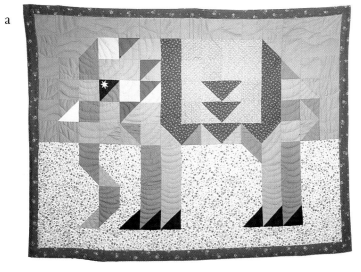

b

e

f

Anca Groves's quilts, also illustrated here, show the art of appliqué taken in a new direction. Her appliquéd characters have a life of their own and seem to dance off the quilts. Anca is a Romanian designer who only recently turned to quilt-making, using the very durable Liberty cotton Tana Lawn prints. Her designs are first drawn on tracing paper and traced on to the appliqué fabric, after which the individual pieces of cotton are cut out and attached together. Then they are machined on to the fabric with great verve. As well as flat cotton Anca sometimes uses satin fabric for objects like balloons, and eyelet for clowns' ruffs. This gives a change of texture which babies will very much enjoy.

To match the quilts, Anca makes pillows and sometimes crib bumpers. A bumper is a good idea for a baby, as it will make him feel more secure and stop him from banging his head against the end of the crib in his sleep and waking himself up. Bumpers are extremely easy to make. Sometimes they are sold to go around one end of a crib only, so you have to switch the bumper if you turn the baby the other way – something that often happens when a baby is teething and gets the sheets wet with dribble at one end. But you can make a bumper that goes right around the cot. For the unusual one-end bumper, just measure the inside end of your crib plus 18–24 in (45–60 cm) at either side, then cut out two lengths of fabric to that length and about 12–18 in (30–45 cm) across. Line the bumper with thickish wadding (about 4-oz) and add a frill as in our picture, or some binding. Add ribbons for attaching it top and bottom at both the corners and at the ends, keeping the ribbons as short as possible. Quilting will help the bumper to stand up, and this is often best done by hand when you are dealing with thick wadding.

Other items can be made to co-ordinate with your quilt and crib bumper – for example diaper stackers, which are simple to contrive yourself but for which you can also buy patterns, and bags and bibs. You can also edge your towels with the same fabric, line baskets and cover tissue holders.

ABOVE: An oval tablecloth made of sheeting material and appliquéd in a vivid mixture of textures and colors. In the center is the gingerbread house, with lollipops and candy canes around.

APPLIQUÉ FABRIC DESIGNS BY ANCA GROVES
OPPOSITE: (a), (b) and (c) Three quilts showing traditional nursery themes used in a totally new way. All of them will make wonderful wall hangings later. (d) This co-ordinated set of quilt, crib bumper, bib and bag is made with much more unusual colors and shades than are traditionally chosen for children's rooms. The finishing touch is provided by appliqué pictures which match the crib linen.

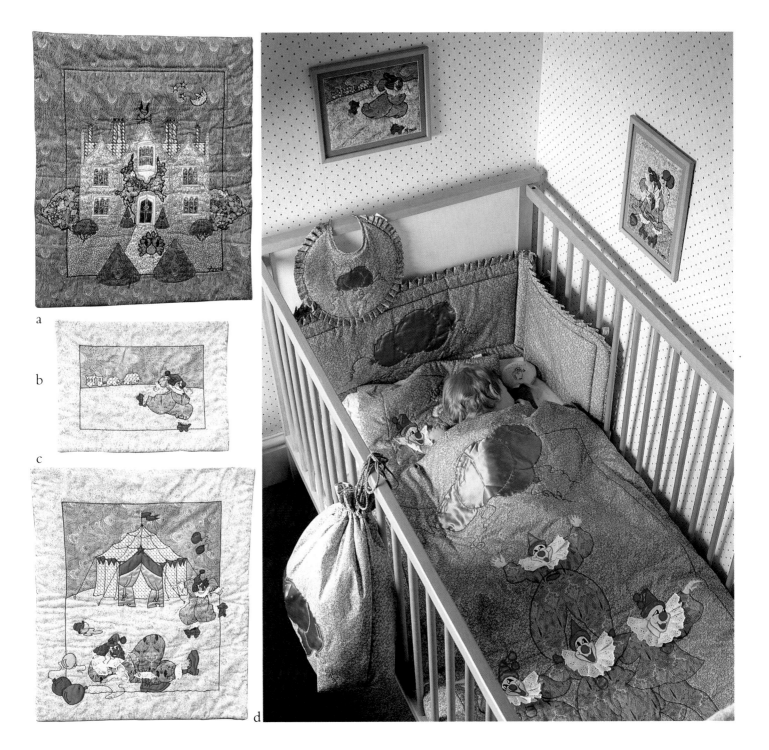

a

b

c

d

141

CUSHIONS

Cushions are not only extremely useful but can also be most decorative in your nursery. They make delightful presents for babies, and somehow you can never have enough. You can make patchwork, appliqué, embroidered, knitted or tapestry cushions. You can create the most exciting designs with fabric paint, either by stenciling or by working freehand on plain cotton cushions. You can also make cushions in the shape of animals, suns and stars. Or you can just make them in basic cushion shapes in a co-ordinating fabric, with either a frill around the edge or a simple binding. We hope our illustrations will give you some ideas.

A birthday pillow painted for a three-year-old boy by his nine-year-old sister, with a bit of advice from an adult. Like many children, Ulick loves parrots and toucans, so these and the tortoise were traced from a book of Edward Lear's birds (by simply putting the book inside the pillow-case) and then painted in fabric paint.

TOP LEFT: A selection of tapestry cushions of animals in very traditional styles, suited to a Victorian style room. These are available in kit form and can also be framed as pictures.

TOP RIGHT: These charming French style cushions, simply made in pastel shades, have been appliquéd to give a third dimension and an interesting texture which fascinates children. The one on the right has a small music box motor which plays a tune when you pull the string. The pink cushion has a child's name embroidered on the balloon.

BOTTOM LEFT: Stenciling and painting can transform the plainest cushions.

BOTTOM RIGHT: This jolly appliquéd cushion has surprises when you open its pockets. Buttons, zippers, Velcro, snaps and ribbon have been added to help children learn these important hand movements. The lucky owner has also been given an A–Z appliqué rag book with jokes on each page.

143

MAKING A TAPESTRY CUSHION

The tabby cat on this tapestry cushion is sewn in cross-stitch on a printed canvas. The canvas, wool and needles are all supplied as a starter pack by Elizabeth Bradley Designs Ltd, and it is simple enough to be made by an older child as a present for a new baby. Alternatively, you could plan your own design or follow one of the many designs published in leaflets and books on needlepoint. The tapestry in this example is 16 in/40 cm square. Below are instructions for mounting a tapestry this size on to a cushion.

MATERIALS
- Your finished piece of needlework
- A piece of backing fabric the same size plus $\frac{1}{2}$ in/ 12 mm border allowance all the way around – velvet, moiré silk and wool fabrics all make good backings
- Sewing machine thread, plus a stronger thread for attaching the cord and tassels
- Cord measuring the circumference of the cushion plus 3 in/7.5 cm extra for turning in the ends
- 4 tassels with cord loops
- 16 in/40 cm feather cushion pad
- 14 in/35 cm zipper (optional)
- Pins and needles
- Scissors
- Cellophane tape

MAKING UP
1 If your needlework piece has been worked in cross-stitch it will not need to be blocked. Just press it on the back with a steam iron and pull it gently into shape.

2 If a different stitch has been used your piece may be misshapen. If so, dampen it slightly, pull it gently into shape, and pin it out on a board with thumbtacks. Leave it to dry thoroughly before using.

3 Trim the edge of the canvas to 1 in/2.5 cm all the way around. Press back the edges with a warm iron.

4 If you are not using a zipper, zigzag stitch along the bottom border of your canvas and backing fabric.

5 If you are using a zipper, this needs to be stitched in place before you make up the cushion. Position it along the bottom edge of the design, and machine sew it to the tapestry and to a border of the backing fabric, with your stitching line as close to the teeth of the zipper as possible.

6 When the zipper is in place, trim the canvas and backing fabric up to the edge of the zipper. Zigzag stitch along the edges (see diagram i).

7 Place the right sides of the tapestry and the backing fabric together. Tack in place. If you are using a zipper, tack around from one end of the zipper to the other. If not, leave a 10 in/25 cm gap at the bottom.

8 Machine stitch around the cushion with the back of the needlework side uppermost. The stitching line should be $\frac{1}{10}$ in/2 mm in from the edge.

144

9 Trim the edges to $\frac{1}{2}$ in/12 mm all the way around. Trim the corners (see diagram ii). Zigzag stitch all the way around.

10 Turn the cushion inside out and push out the corners.

11 Press gently with a damp cloth.

12 Insert the cushion pad.

13 If no zipper has been used, the gap must now be stitched up. Use strong thread and sew as shown (see diagram iii). After every 5 or 6 stitches pull the thread tight. Leave a small hole at one end of the gap for the cord ends to be tucked into. If you have used a zipper, make a small hole at one end of it.

14 Push one end of the cord into the hole and stitch in place. Attach the cord to your cushion as neatly as possible, using small stitches. Do not pull the cord tight or the cushion will pucker. Keep your stitches shallow or you may sew into the feather pad.

15 When you have stitched the cord all the way around, cut it, leaving about 1 in/2.5 cm to push into the hole. Bind the end with cellophane tape and push it into the hole. Stitch it into place.

16 Thread the cord loops of the tassels on to the trimming cord at each corner of the cushion, and stitch into place.

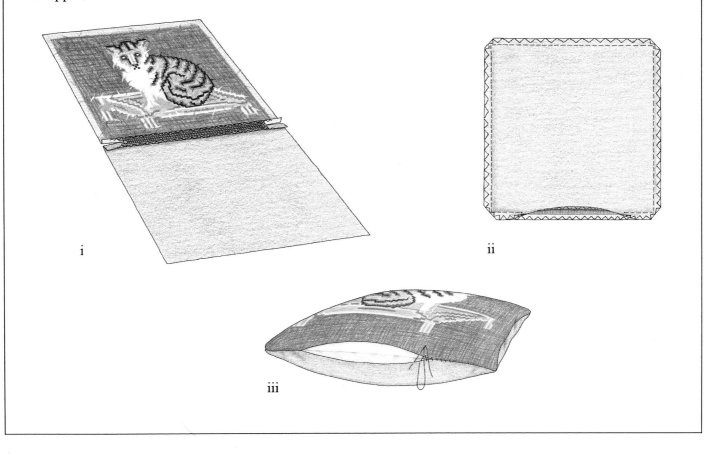

i

ii

iii

———————

WINDOW ON THE WORLD

Lighting is all-important in a child's room. You will want to make the most of all the natural light available, while ensuring that the room can be dark for nap times. When evening comes and artificial light takes over, the room should look as cozy as possible while making certain that the child has enough good light to play by.

WINDOWS

There are many different ways to treat windows, the most obvious choices being curtains, shutters and blinds. Whatever you do, remember that in the early years it is crucial to keep out the light when your baby is asleep. As he gets older you will be grateful for those dark curtains, without which he would wake himself – and you – at 5 a.m. To achieve a darkened room you need not have heavy curtains or shutters. Any good large fabric store will sell lightproof curtain lining and blackout blind material, which can be white. The curtains on p. 97 are lined in blackout lining. Any kind of lining has the added bonus of providing some soundproofing.

CURTAINS

Before selecting your fabric you must decide what sort of curtains you want. Highly elaborate curtains are not appropriate for children's rooms, nor is it sensible to have curtains that reach down to the floor, as they will only get covered in fingerprints, be used as hiding places and eventually be pulled down. This does not mean that you cannot have interesting window treatments.

A simple pair of gathered curtains, with a gathered valance in the same fabric, can be dressed up or down. For English Country rooms they should be left just as

Here the bay window has been made into a wonderfully cozy corner of the room. The curtain valance has scalloped edges which have been trimmed in pink, and the tie-backs are also scalloped with rosettes. The window seat and cushions in matching fabric give unity to the setting.

they are, with perhaps some contrasting binding, whereas in a more elaborate Victorian room you could add lace to the edges or a frill in the same material and introduce some sophistication with tie-backs. Binding the edge of a plain curtain in a co-ordinating color can make it stand out from the wall and look most striking. Simple gathered curtains look best with a valance.

You can create interesting effects with a valance. In a more modern room, dispense with the frills and have flat or box pleats on the valance. Fabric valances cut in shapes such as scallops can look charming, or you could choose a plain wooden valance, either covered in the curtain fabric or painted in matching or contrasting colors. Wooden valances can also be cut out in interesting shapes. In a Modern Romantic room you might select the Man in the Moon or some other character.

Curtains can look very attractive hanging from wooden rods. These curtain rods have large wooden rings from which the curtains are suspended. Here no valence is used, so the pleats actually show. You can have ordinary gathered pleats, or you might do pinch pleats or single goblet pleats, placing the pleat where the curtain joins the ring. Curtain rods are appropriate for the simpler styles, such as American Country and Scandinavian.

ABOVE: An easy and economical way of decorating curtains is by stenciling on to plain fabric. Here, farmyard animals caper across plain chintz curtains. The stencils are pre-cut, and were applied with fabric stencil paint then heat-sealed with a warm iron.

LEFT: With its co-ordinated curtain and blind fabric, neat tie-backs and pleated valance, this window set makes a most attractive focal point for a little girl's town nursery.

When selecting your fabric, don't restrict yourself to furnishing fabrics. Dress fabrics can make lovely curtains so long as you line them to give them body. (Many dress fabrics are not treated to resist sunlight, however, so it is probably best not to use them for the windows of a south-facing room.) Plain unbleached calico makes marvelous curtains which cost very little. It is ideal for Scandinavian, English Country or American Country rooms, and can be stenciled or embroidered for extra interest. Sheeting, again very reasonably priced, also makes excellent curtains when lined, and is a good background for appliqué, stenciling or freehand painting. Children as young as five or six will enjoy painting on curtain fabric. Patchwork or appliquéd curtains are tremendous fun to make and can easily be machine sewn.

BELOW LEFT: These wonderfully romantic curtains have been made in butter muslin. They are swagged and tailed on the valance and then bunched at the side. The blind is made of a white blackout fabric, and the painting is done with emulsion paint colored with food coloring.

BELOW RIGHT: This delightful curtain made of unbleached calico was painted by a group of five- and six-year-olds using fabric pens, which are very easy to use. A project like this needs supervision, and could be done with older siblings, perhaps to help prepare for the new baby.

BLINDS

Curtains can look really striking when combined with blinds. The blinds add the practical bonus of screening out more light. Shades can be of the simple plain-colored roller variety, contrasting with the curtains, or you can buy a plain blind and paint it either with delightful flowers to co-ordinate with your room scheme, or with a bold illustration – for example, a Humpty Dumpty who will sit on the window-sill when you pull the blind down.

Country style gathered valance

Victorian style shaped valance

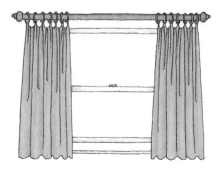

French style scalloped heading

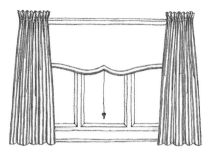

Unlined curtains with blind

Romantic style Austrian blind

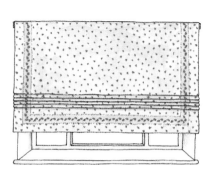

Now Look Roman blind

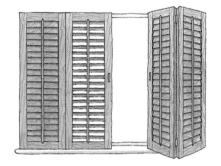

Exotic style wooden shutters

Scandinavian style painted shutters

Stenciled shutters

WINDOW TREATMENTS

Festoon blinds, which are very popular now, are more romantic and look appropriate in Victorian Nostalgic, French or Modern Romantic rooms. Roman blinds are made of fabric and pleat upwards. They are very elegant, and if made in an Indian or Thai fabric would be appropriate for an Exotic room. Bamboo blinds would also be just right for the Exotic room.

Venetian blinds have a rather tacky reputation. But they can look very stylish indeed nowadays and, so long as your child cannot play with the cords, they would be ideal for the Now Look. These days instead of the usual boring gray they come in bright colors as well.

SHUTTERS

Shutters are marvelous for keeping out the late evening light in northern countries like Sweden, and for keeping out the heat in southern climates like France, Italy and the southern states of America. Southern American houses often have shutters – frequently the charming old-style plantation shutters which can be closed completely or half closed to let in a dappled light. The shutters and the window frame can be painted in an interesting color to emphasize or contrast with the color of the room. Shutters can also be painted with charming scenes to entertain your child, or decorated with stencils as they so often are in American and Scandinavian rooms.

LIGHTS

When planning a lighting scheme, think first of safety. No light must be within reach of a small child or he will explore its contents and risk an electric shock. Nor should you use bedside lamps which plug in, as these can easily be pulled off or knocked off a table. For the first few years the best solution is overhead lights, in the form of spots, central hanging lights or wall lights well out of reach. Even with these restrictions there are quite a lot of exciting options open to you.

Remember that you will want to vary the lighting in a room, ranging from a bright light to play by to the very dim light that some children require for sleep. Dimmer switches are a godsend. Avoid scary lighting that creates strange shadows and might frighten a child.

CENTRAL LIGHTS

There are many delightful lampshades for children on the market, and choosing them can be fun. The ubiquitous round paper fold-up ones come in many patterns, and are so cheap that you can change them quite often. But there are more unusual and exotic ones to be obtained from shops specializing in Eastern goods. Seek out beautiful paper shades from Japan and China, and bamboo and reeded ones from many parts of Asia. Oriental shops may also sell wooden bird cages, which are not expensive, and can look delightful converted into lights, as on p. 157.

Always choose shapes that will suit the style of your nursery: plain bright geometric ones for the Now Look, hot air balloons for Modern Romantic, eyelet or lace for Victorian, and perhaps an interesting wooden or wrought-iron chandelier in a Scandinavian room. For the French look, a lampshade to co-ordinate with your color scheme is a must.

You can have great fun painting lampshades, using fabric paint on plain white fabric shades in any style you choose. Paper lampshades can also be painted. Sponge or colour-wash the shade, using a water-based paint. You can also stencil lampshades, using either the brush or the spray technique.

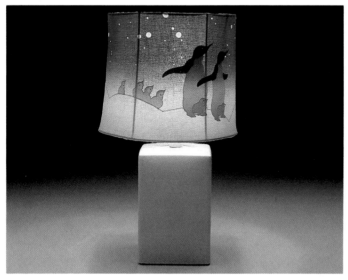

Old-fashioned brass wall lights are particularly appropriate for the Victorian look, harking back to the days of gas lights. In Scandinavian rooms, where candles were so much a part of life, you could even have some interesting side lights with fake candles on carved sconces.

TABLE LIGHTS

Once you are sure the child is old enough, say from five or six years onwards, then you can risk a table light, making sure that the cord is concealed so that it can't be tripped over. Also make sure that the base of the lamp is very stable. Now you can opt for more interesting lampshades; they will be much more visible, and their details will intrigue a small child.

TOP LEFT: A simple, cheap lampshade, bought for a modern room. The designs, inspired by Alexander Calder, were drawn with fabric pens.

MIDDLE LEFT: These rabbit and moon lamps cast a lovely glow and are very evocative. They also look very attractive as ornaments by day.

BOTTOM LEFT: This lampshade is executed with such wonderful detail that it seems a waste to have it as a central light. Far better to use it as a bedside lamp, where it can be looked at closely. The background fabric and the penguins were painted separately, and the penguins then appliquéd on to the background using tiny stitches. The shade was also lined with white fabric.

MAKING A SET OF PAINTED CURTAINS

This room was rather long, so it needed as much light as possible. We made white sheeting curtains, differentiating them from the white walls by binding the edges in green, and decided to paint them. The aim was to keep them very simple, echoing the bright colors and circus theme of the rest of the room.

MATERIALS

– *Curtains*: the amount of sheeting you need obviously depends on the size of your window. First estimate the length of the curtains by measuring from the top of the curtain rod to a few inches below the sill and adding 6 in/15 cm for the curtain hem and heading. Then measure the width of the curtain rod and add 6 in/15 cm if you wish the curtains to overlap at the center. Multipy this by $1\frac{1}{2}$, which gives the total width of the curtains before gathering. Divide the total width by the width of the sheeting, rounding it up to the nearest full number to estimate how many widths of fabric the curtains will take. (For instance, if the total width of the finished curtains is 132 in/330 cm, you will need three widths of sheeting 45 in/115 cm wide.) To calculate the actual length of sheeting to buy, multiply the number of widths by the curtain length, including upper and lower hems.

– *Valance frill*: you will need strips of sheeting which, when sewn together, give twice the width of the valance and a depth of about 9 in/23 cm, allowing $\frac{1}{2}$ in/12 mm for seams (i.e. those joining the widths of sheeting together plus the upper and lower hems).

– *Lining*: to ensure darkness at night, use white blackout fabric. You will need the same quantity of fabric as for the sheeting, but each width will be about 7 in/17.5 cm shorter. The valance frill can be lined with sheeting, cut to exactly the same size.

– *Binding*: dark green bias binding at least 4 times the length of the finished curtains, plus the length of the pelmet frill.

– *Gathering tape*: you will need a length of gathering tape measuring the total width of the curtains, as calculated above, plus 2 in/5 cm for turning back.

– Curtain hooks

– Velcro (finished width of the valance frill)

– Fabric glue

– Needles

– Pins

– Scissors

– Thread (white and dark green)

– Felt-tipped pens for fabric, or fabric paints to use with a suitably-sized brush

- Measuring tape
- Scrap paper
- Newspaper
- Pencil
- Iron

MAKING UP

1 Following the measurements above, cut out the requisite number of widths. If you are using three widths, fold one width in half along its length and cut along the fold. Pin together one width with one half width (see diagram i), but first oversew the edges to be joined. Machine together, stitching $\frac{1}{2}$ in/ 12 mm from the edge, and press the seam open. For the hem, turn up the lower edge by 1 in/2.5 cm and press; turn up once more by 2 in/5 cm, press and then hem-stitch by hand. Repeat with the other width/half width.

2 Join the widths of blackout material as in (**1**) – there is no need to hem this fabric.

3 Place the sheeting and lining with reverse sides together, with the top of the lining 3 in/7.5 cm from the top of the sheeting, 1 in/2.5 cm from the bottom, and the side edges together (see diagram ii). Pin the side edges together and machine stitch $\frac{1}{2}$ in/ 12 mm from the edge. The lower edges of the sheeting and lining are not joined, so that the lining hangs loose and prevents the sheeting from puckering.

4 To make the upper curtain hem, turn over the sheeting by $\frac{1}{2}$ in/12 mm and press; turn over again so that the fabric folds over the top of the lining, press and hem-stitch by hand (see diagram iii).

5 Pin the bias binding to the long, vertical edge of each curtain, the reverse side of the binding against

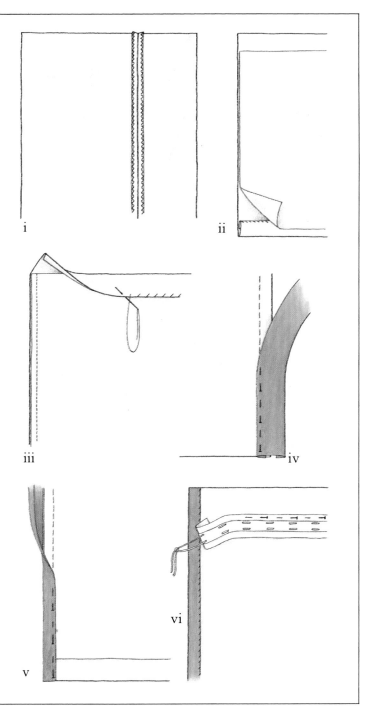

i

ii

iii

iv

v

vi

154

the right side of the curtain and covering up the line of stitching joining the sheeting to the lining (see diagram iv). Using a seam of $\frac{5}{8}$ in/1.5 cm, machine-stitch the binding to each of the four edges, fold it over, enclosing the raw edges of the sheeting and the lining, and pin the free edge of the binding to the lining, again covering up the original seam (see diagram v). Machine-stitch or hem the binding to the reverse side of the curtain, turning in the raw edges of the binding at each end of the curtain.

6 Take a piece of gathering tape cut to the required length for one curtain, and with a pin draw out about 1 in/2.5 cm of the cords from each end of the tape, in order to allow for turnings. Knot the cords together on the wrong side at one end of the tape, and knot them loosely together on the right side at the other end. Place the tape along the top hem of the curtain, its top edge about $1\frac{1}{2}$ in/4 cm from the top of the curtain, with the loosely knotted edge aligned with the outer edge of the curtain. Turn under 1 in/2.5 cm of the tape at each end and pin the upper edge of the tape to the curtain (see diagram vi). Stitch the upper edge of the tape to the curtain and repeat with the lower edge. Follow the same steps for the second curtain.

7 Cut out the valance frill and lining from the sheeting. Pin these together along three sides, leaving one long edge free. Machine stitch the three edges together, using a seam of $\frac{1}{2}$ in/12 mm. Trim the corners, turn inside out and press. Pin together the remaining edges and sew together with a seam of $\frac{1}{2}$ in/12 mm. Following the instructions in (5), attach bias binding to this edge only to form the lower edge of the valance frill. The curtains and valance frill are now ready to be painted.

CURTAIN PAINTING
1 Make a rough drawing on paper first, and practice with the fabric paints on some scraps of sheeting until you are satisfied with your design. We have used a circus theme here, but illustrations in children's books are a good source of ideas for simple, bold designs. If you are not confident about your drawing ability, simple shapes like spirals and zigzags can be equally effective.

2 Spread some paper on the floor and lay the curtains right side up on top. Draw the basic outlines of your design very faintly in pencil. Then begin applying the fabric paints, starting with the larger shapes. Add smaller motifs, too, so that the curtains "tell a story" when they are drawn open as well as closed. Repeat the smaller motifs on the valance frill. Leave to dry.

3 Taking one finished curtain, draw up the cord in the gathering tape from the loosely-knotted end to fit the curtain rod, space the gathers evenly and insert curtain hooks at intervals. Knot the drawn-up cords to hold them in position and tie up the slack into a bow. Repeat with the second curtain and attach both to the curtain rod.

4 Make even pleats along the upper edge of the valance frill (see the illustration), pressing these and pinning them in place. Machine stitch along the upper edge of the frill to anchor the pleats.

5 Cut a strip of Velcro to equal the finished width of the valance frill and separate the two halves. Pin one strip to the upper edge of the frill on the reverse side and machine the upper and lower edge of the Velcro to the frill. Place the second strip along the upper edge of the valance, attaching it with glue. Wait for this to dry before attaching the frill.

Chapter Fourteen

BRINGING THE WALLS TO LIFE

Whether your child's nursery is a tiny cubbyhole at the top of the house or a large airy bedroom, what you do to the walls can transform it into something altogether more exciting. So before you embark, think hard about what you want the room to look like. Will what looks ideal for your newborn baby suit a boisterous three-year-old? If not, are you prepared to do a major redecoration then, or will you try and achieve a look that can somehow be dressed up later? Your range of choices is enormous, and here are some.

PAINT

The simplest option you have is to leave the walls quite plain and paint them one color. For this, use either an emulsion paint which is water-based, or a matte or silk vinyl, both of which are easier to clean. The advantages of a plain-colored wall are that there is a vast range of colors to choose from and that you have enormous freedom in the kind of furniture, pictures, hangings, curtains and window treatments you use. Painting is also a very cheap form of decoration. The main disadvantage is that plain colors show the dirt much more than patterned surfaces, so a toddler's grubby fingers will leave their mark. While paint is wipable, it is not scrubbable.

Of course you need not paint the walls with just a simple matte surface. Today the old techniques of ragging, sponging, color-washing and combing are popular again, and with good reason. They all create interesting warm effects and a pleasing illusion of depth. Walls can be sponged with emulsion paint, but for the best results it is worth taking the time and effort to use oil paint and glaze over an eggshell paint surface. This is a lengthier

*This town house playroom has been transformed with a painted tree, with fruit, birds and animals
in the branches. The hatchway has been disguised to look like two windows of a neighboring
house.*

process, but the result looks more professional and is more hard-wearing. The glaze can also be wiped and washed. If in addition you varnish it with polyurethane, it creates an excellent protection against the ravages of children. For instructions on ragging, sponging and dragging, see p. 170–71.

If you want more decoration than just a painted wall, a good alternative is to paint the wall and use wallpaper borders around the top of the walls and perhaps around the windows and door. You could also buy or make curtains to match the border. This is a cheap and easy way to achieve instant co-ordination.

Stenciled borders are another option – you can buy ready-made stencils or cut them out yourself. When you gain confidence you can actually design your own stencils, taking themes from much-loved children's books or favorite toys.

A hand-painted border, painted either freehand or using templates to create a geometric pattern, can be very effective. You can also create an exciting border using vegetable prints. Borders of this kind are quick and easy to make with either potatoes, carrots or rutabagas, and the blocked effect gives a simple, childlike look. Don't feel obliged to do a figurative motif. Try an abstract pattern of circles, dots and crosses, and don't worry if the print is not quite perfect – as long as they are not serious, the imperfections will make the border all the more interesting.

WALLPAPER

Children's wallpapers today can be a delight. There is a huge variety, and if you go to a good shop you will be overwhelmed by the choices – there are excellent designs from America and Britain, France and Italy, many sold with matching or co-ordinating borders and fabrics for curtains and bedspreads. Most children's wallpapers are in washable vinyl which, while it cannot be really scrubbed, can at least be wiped clean. If the wallpaper you use is not washable, you can protect it with a coat of clear varnish. When selecting your paper it is best to avoid recognizable cartoon favorites from TV or films, which may well be out of favor with the occupant of the room next year and which have a strong tendency to become dated. A lovely wallpaper can be the main focus for a room and some children's wallpapers are surprisingly cheap; remember, though, that the cost of hanging them can mount up. The only real snag about wallpaper is that it can tear easily.

MURALS

A mural can create a delightful and exciting atmosphere in the most unpromising space. Suddenly the room will seem altogether bigger, as the lines of the corners and ceiling dissolve and your eye is taken to wider vistas. Murals are quite taxing to do, of course, and for the more complicated ones you do need painting flair and expertise. But you can also create delightful effects very simply. Even for the amateur decorator, it is definitely an idea worth exploring.

OPPOSITE: A charming and evocative mural of children at play painted around the doorway to a nursery. The artist, Charles Mackesy, specializes in representing children in a manner that will appeal to all age groups.

The best paints to use for murals are acrylic, tempera and children's watercolor paints, and for these you will need a base of vinyl silk emulsion on a flat, well-prepared wall. You can also use an eggshell base, particularly if you are going to use spray paint (see p. 163). When the mural is complete and dry it is sensible, though not absolutely essential, to add a varnish to protect it. The most durable varnish is polyurethane, but this has the disadvantage of yellowing the paint somewhat. Emulsion varnish will not change the paint color, but it is not as strong.

If all four walls are to be painted with murals, you must be sure to choose a theme which will not be too overpowering and claustrophobic. A gentle, open-air scene is the most suitable. Try a sea scene, complete with ships, yachts, fishing boats, whales and fish and, on the shore, beaches and a lighthouse. Another good all-around idea is a road, with buses, cars and bicycles, which winds around the room, sometimes disappearing behind hills and trees. For a small room, a sky with hot-air balloons, kites, birds, airplanes and rockets would give a soft effect.

A pond makes a wonderfully tranquil setting. You can create a water effect with frottage (see p. 164), and then print the grasses and reeds using the edge of a piece of cardboard. For extra interest, paint a child fishing in a row boat among ducks and swans, with frogs on lily pads, fish, bulrushes and dragonflies in the foreground.

TOP LEFT: This dramatic scene with Captain Hook's ship from Peter Pan *makes ingenious use of the shape of the room and its beams. The chest at the end of the bed carries the theme into the room.*
LEFT: The blue and green fabric, also used in the curtains, and the car-shaped bed have provided a theme and a color scheme for this imaginative mural.

For a mural using a river theme you could use the same basis and include characters from *The Wind in the Willows*. More suited to an older child would be a jungle scene with exotic flora and fauna. If you choose to do this, however, be careful not to make it too dark and menacing. Leaf shapes can be applied quickly using large potatoes and even carrots cut lengthwise.

Picnic scenes are very popular with small children. They can be set beside a pond or stream, in open country or a woodland glade. Children take great delight in pretending to eat the cheese or the cherries on the cakes. The best picnic of all was the Mad Hatter's tea party in *Alice in Wonderland*, and it is a perfect subject for a mural.

Rather than painting an all-around design, you may prefer to have a mural on just one wall. This way you can use the other three walls for your child's paintings, pictures, hangings and bookshelves. It is fun to choose something that tells a story. Tales from literary favorites such as Beatrix Potter and A. A. Milne are popular with small children, and make for gentle-looking murals. Bolder and more exciting schemes like Noah's ark give you a marvelous opportunity to use exotic animals. Closer to home, a farmyard complete with hens, ducks, geese, pigs and cows and a shady tree will absorb and fascinate your child. A tree painted in the corner of the room and spreading up into the ceiling can create a glorious effect (see p. 157) and will provide an excellent setting for birds, flowers and animals.

ABOVE RIGHT: The sky theme in this small bedroom gives a feeling of space. A small air vent high on the wall was covered up by turning it into the basket of the hot-air balloon.

RIGHT: This simple Singing in the Rain *mural makes bathtime more exciting. The walls were sprayed with blue paint and the score was painted on top.*

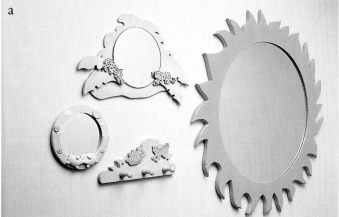

(d) *Painted in smoky colors with a dash of gold, this romantic boy and his dappled horse give a quite magical look to a plain nursery wall.*

(e) *This delightful stencil of circus cats was applied using the brush method.*

(a) *These mirrors, made with charming wooden cut-out frames and spray painted, are excellent for stimulating the imagination of young children.*

(b) *and* (c) *A clock in a child's room not only encourages him to learn his letters and the time; it can also look wonderful. These charming clocks are made of painted plywood and use a simple battery operated mechanism.*

162

When planning your mural and sketching it out, be sure to avoid using large objects. Remember that what may seem a normal size to you can look like a giant to a small child. Don't use strong or dark colors, which can dominate and frighten, and don't paint frightening faces on animals or people, as they can cause nightmares. If in doubt, aim at a smile. Try to include small items, which will be the subject of many imaginative games: for example, paint ladybugs or snails hidden in the grasses. Introduce small unexpected details, such as a tiny mouse eating cheese in a corner. As you plan, think of how you might use the mural to tell a story, and include enough visual detail to enable the child to create stories for himself and his friends.

While the colors do not have to be pastel, avoid too many bright, intense colors – these will quickly overpower even a large nursery. Soft pastels are very suitable for a newborn, but a two-year-old will expect something more robust. Choose clean, clear colors, and avoid shading unless you are an experienced painter. Shapes and brush-strokes should be clearly delineated, so that there will be no confusion in the child's mind as to the shape and identity of the different elements of your design. Keep the colors flat, and avoid anything but the most simple perspectives.

Restrict your palette to no more than six to eight colors – for example, two greens, one red, two blues, one or two yellows and a white. A child must be able to identify the colors, so avoid neutral browns or grays. Red is usually the first color a child recognizes, so try to include it. Aim to keep the colors in the same tonal range. Before you start your mural, try out each color on a spare piece of paper. Half close your eyes and make sure that no color looks too dark, unless it is a special detail.

MURAL SHORT CUTS

Although elaborate hand-painted murals are exciting, few of us have the time or the expertise to create them. So here are some short cuts.

SPRAY CANS

This is a very cheap and simple way of creating a soft and interesting effect. You can easily make a charming spray sky using an ozone-friendly household spray paint. Cut out paper templates of birds, secure them on a white wall with Blu-tak or spray adhesive, then spray the paint around the templates. When the paint is dry, remove the templates and you will find a delightful result. Spray paint can also be used with stencils to make interesting shapes and, with masking tape, to mark the outlines of your design. You can spray on seas, hills and trees. The only problem with this method is that spray paint makes a dreadful smell and you have to wear a mask while applying it. Pregnant women should not use it, and children must be kept out of the room until the paint is absolutely dry and the fumes have completely gone. When you are spraying, all furniture and carpets in the room must be covered up. Open the windows as wide as possible to help the fumes to disperse.

SPONGES

Use a natural sponge to create the effect of foliage in trees and to make a mottled grass effect. Just dip the sponge lightly in the wet paint, and dab it onto the wall to create foliage. For grass, apply the paint normally then quickly dab it with the sponge to remove a bit and create a mottled texture.

CORK ENDS

Cork ends are good for making quick and easy spots. Just apply paint to them and dab them on to the wall. They can be used to make flower centers and petals, car wheels or leopard spots. Cut-out synthetic sponge can be used in the same way to create more elaborate shapes such as stars, triangles and crescents.

CARDBOARD

Pieces of cardboard can be used as templates to create shapes of houses, cars and trains. Narrow pieces will make long straight lines for fences, tree trunks and railway tracks.

MASKING TAPE

This is used to mask any areas you do not wish to paint or spray. You can use it to make stripes and edgings. But do not apply it to delicate paint surfaces, and be sure not to leave it on the wall for long because it may remove the paint or wallpaper underneath.

ROLLER

A small paint roller can be used to make long lines or stripes – perfect for roads, lanes and rivers.

FROTTAGE

This is a very quick and effective method of creating a special paint effect over a large area. Apply a liberal coating of paint, then soak up the excess by placing a piece of matte brown paper over it and rubbing gently. This creates a varied texture which is very effective for water and for green hills.

PAPER CUT-OUTS

This is an excitingly versatile method of making a mural. First paint a basic landscape with hills, a few trees and sky. Then cut out balloons, birds, cars and houses out of brightly colored paper and stick them on to the landscape with either double-sided tape or Blu-tak. When the cut-outs get shabby you can replace them with a new and different set of designs. This is the sort of enterprise that all the family can be involved in.

TEMPLATES

As well as making good friezes, these can be used in murals to create starlit skies and many other scenes (see illustrations opposite). Ready-made templates can be bought in many craft stores and children's shops, or you can make your own from stiff cardboard.

PAINTS TO USE FOR MURALS

There are many types of paints you can use. Artists' acrylic colors, though expensive, are wonderful, and so are tempera paints. Avoid poster paint or gouache, as it is not washable and will run and smudge if splashed. Children's quick-drying watercolor paint is excellent. It comes in a good range of colors and is cheap and easy to obtain. The colors are rather cruder than acrylics, but this can be quite appropriate for children's murals. Raid your children's paints and crayons, including their non-washable felt-tipped pens.

SIMPLE ACRYLIC PAINT EFFECTS FOR NURSERY WALLS
(a) These red and blue boats were made using potato prints. The wavy line was made with a felt-tipped pen, and the rest of the wall was combed to create a checked effect.
(b) Over a yellow painted wall, a checkerboard effect was drawn with a waterproof felt-tipped pen. The clown was sculpted out of bread dough and baked, then painted and varnished.
(c) Yellow acrylic paint was painted along the edge of a length of masking tape. The yellow dots were put on with the end of a cork.
(d) A simple clown shape was cut out on a folded strip of paper and used as a reverse stencil. The red border was painted using two strips of masking tape.
(e) The flat surface of a synthetic sponge was cut out in a house shape using a sharp craft knife. Paint was applied to the sponge and then printed on the wall.
(f) Star motifs made from a star-shaped potato cut-out.

165

PAINTING A LANDSCAPE MURAL

You do not need to be an expert painter to create a landscape mural like the one illustrated here. However, you do need plenty of time and you should not undertake a project like this, which involves the use of spray paint for the sky, if you are pregnant, as the paint fumes are toxic. You must also keep children away from the room until the fumes have dispersed and the paint is completely dry. Before you start, remove as much furniture as possible and protect the floor and anything that can't be moved with drop cloths. Open the windows to help disperse the paint fumes.

There is no need to buy expensive artists'-quality paint and brushes. Children's paint, brushes and paper are much cheaper and just as effective for murals of this kind. Acrylic paint has been used here on the trees and houses, etc., as it is more permanent than watercolor.

MATERIALS
– For the sky: pale blue spray paint
– For the grass: children's ready-mixed paint in squeeze bottles, though these have a limited range of colors. Use green on its own or mix it with blue for a darker shade. In this example, both shades have been used to vary the color.
– For the trees and houses: acrylic paint in yellow ochre and white for the house walls; crimson and raw umber for the roofs; oxide of chromium and emerald green for the trees; raw umber and burnt siena for the trunks
– Protective mask
– 4 in/10 cm and 8 in/20 cm paintbrushes
– Chubby children's paintbrushes
– Fine nylon brush
– Natural sponge
– Newspaper
– Colored paper
– Small square and rectangular cardboard boxes or cartons
– Wallpaper glue
– Crayons
– Polyurethane varnish and varnish brush (optional)

METHOD
1 Make sure all the wall surfaces are in good condition. White emulsion, satinwood finish and eggshell paint all make suitable bases for murals. Avoid gloss paint.
2 Clear the room of all furniture or cover it with drop cloths.
3 Wearing a protective mask, spray the ceiling and the top two thirds of the walls with spray paint. Follow the manufacturer's instructions and apply

the paint very sparingly, leaving some areas almost white to create a cloud-like effect. Leave overnight to dry. A fine dust will be left everywhere, so you will need to vacuum the room.

4 Apply the mixed paints for the hills with an 8 in/20 cm paintbrush, working as quickly as possible. Start by painting an undulating line to simulate rolling hillsides, and work downwards with quick, overlapping brushstrokes, making sure the whole area is covered. Use dark and lighter green areas to provide variety.

5 Before the paint is dry, use a sheet of newspaper to mop up any excess. This will give an interesting mottled texture, in keeping with the spray sky.

6 For the trees, houses and balloons, the following short-cut methods create attractive, childlike results:

Trees: for the trunks, brush brown acrylic paint on to one side of a long cardboard box such as a toothpaste carton, then use it to print the tree trunks on the wall. For the leaves, dip a damp sponge into a mixture of emerald green and oxide of chromium acrylic paint, and dab the sponge on top of the trunks.

Houses: follow the same printing technique as for the trees but use square or rectangular boxes. Use a fine paintbrush and acrylic paint to add details such as windows, doors, roofs and chimneys.

Balloons: use the same methods as above, using circular pieces of cardboard, or cut oval shapes from colored paper and stick them on to the wall with wallpaper glue. Draw the balloon strings with a crayon or with fine lines of acrylic paint.

Other details: Small details such as fencing, flowers and birds can all be added, using acrylic paint and a fine paintbrush.

7 When the mural is completely dry, you can give it two coats of clear polyurethane varnish, allowing plenty of time for the first coat to dry before applying the second layer. This is not absolutely necessary, but does give the mural extra protection.

Chapter Fifteen

THE PAINT BOX

For centuries people have decorated furniture with paint. It is a tradition which is not confined to children's furniture, though because of its potential for amusing designs, personalized chairs and headboards it is particularly popular with children. All the styles and traditions we have mentioned in this book use painted furniture, with an extraordinarily varied range of methods and effects.

In the past paint was sometimes used, as it often is today, to conceal the poor quality or the general hodgepodge of the wood underneath, or it was used to give a general uniformity to a mixture of ill-matched pieces. This particularly applied in the American settler communities, where good furniture was scarce. And this necessity gave rise to some of the most brilliant painted furniture ever created. Furniture painted specifically for children only became popular at the turn of this century.

In Britain simple pieces were painted white with illustrations of Peter Rabbit and other favorite characters. Companies like Dragons still do variations on this style. Peter de Wit has developed a more eclectic and robust style, while Moyra Bannister has drawn on her Scandinavian background to produce more lushly individual pieces.

Today, paint is often used to give a lively co-ordinated look to a modern nursery and in certain cases to create the most amusing pieces of furniture. Professionally hand-painted furniture can command high prices, but if you have the time to spare, you can redeem cheap, second-hand pieces with a simple paintwork scheme.

When you paint furniture yourself it is really important to prepare it well before you start. If you are painting old or second-hand furniture it is important to have it stripped before you begin. Hardwoods like oak and

This painted furniture was created by Moyra Bannister, an artist of Swedish origin. There is a strong Swedish tradition of making and painting items to celebrate family events. The chest of drawers was a wedding present to the artist's daughter.

mahogany are better surfaces than pine, because they are not so easily dented and damaged when knocked. If you can have the furniture stripped professionally and cheaply, so much the better. (This especially applies to bulky pieces of furniture, as paint-stripping is a messy and time-consuming process.) If you are doing it yourself you must then strip off all the old paint and varnish, because if you paint on top of an old surface the new paint will chip off. Use either a brush-on paint and varnish remover or one of the newer paste-like substances which are spread on, allowed to dry and then peeled off. The fumes are toxic, so avoid doing it yourself if you are pregnant. If the varnish has long disappeared and any paint left is firmly stuck, use a medium sanding block to roughen the surface very slightly and remove any lumps and bumps so that the new paint will stick. Another reason why it is important to remove old paint is that it often contains a lot of lead, which is dangerous if chewed by children. Modern paint contains very little lead and sometimes none at all. Read the label on the paint can before you buy it.

CHOOSING YOUR PAINT

The type of paint you select will depend very much on the final effect you wish to achieve. Gloss paint would not be suited to a Scandinavian or American Country look, but could be ideal for a bright red chair in a modern nursery. Eggshell is a good paint to use – it has a medium sheen which is neither glossy nor flat, and it is easily wiped clean. You can also use emulsion paint, which has the advantage of being quick-drying, but to protect it you would have to apply a varnish afterwards. When it comes to detailed decoration you can use acrylic paint which is rather tactile and should be varnished when dry for complete protection. Gouache or poster paint must be varnished or it will wash off. On an eggshell or gloss base it is better to use oil color, but remember that this will take a very long time to dry. For stenciling you may use specialty stencil paints, acrylics or spray paint on top of eggshell or emulsion.·

GLAZED PAINT FINISHES

Paint glazes create distinctive and lasting effects that can transform cheap pieces of furniture and will not be outgrown by your child. Some glazed paint finishes are too sophisticated for children's rooms, but dragged, ragged and sponged pieces can happily stand in Victorian, Scandinavian and Modern Romantic style nurseries.

A glazed paint finish is a clear glaze, tinted with artists' oil colors, which is applied so as to "float" on an eggshell basecoat. The color of the glaze should relate quite closely to that of the eggshell base; otherwise the result will be unnaturally crude and startling. All glazed paint finishes will benefit from the protection of two or three coats of clear polyurethane varnish.

SPONGING

Sponged effects can be created quite simply and speedily by dipping a small, natural sponge into a tinted oil glaze mixture and dabbing it on to the eggshell basecoat. Before you start, dip your sponge in clean water and squeeze out any excess moisture. Start at the top of the piece of furniture and work outwards and downwards, taking care not to let the sponge become too saturated with the glaze. When you have finished, rinse out the sponge first in turpentine, then in warm, soapy water.

For extra depth, apply a second layer of glaze once the first layer has had time to dry.

RAGGING

Ragged paint finishes are achieved by applying a tinted oil glaze over an eggshell basecoat with a household paintbrush, then breaking up the glaze with rags to reveal the color beneath. For a harmonious result, use an oil glaze that is slightly darker than the color of the basecoat. The kind of effect you create will be dictated by the type of rag you use. Choose a cotton rag for a soft, regular effect; crinkled plastic or paper bags for a looser, bolder result. Work outwards and downwards from the top of the piece of furniture. If you are ragging a large item, proceed one step at a time, glazing and then ragging an area of about a yard; otherwise the glaze may dry before you have ragged it.

DRAGGING

Dragged paint finishes are achieved by applying a tinted oil glaze on to an eggshell basecoat with a household paintbrush in vertical stripes, then dragging a flogging brush through the glaze with swift, vertical strokes. Flogging brushes are fairly expensive, unfortunately, but small items can also be dragged using a cotton rag. Work with the grain of the wood, and wipe any excess paint off the brush if it becomes too clogged.

STARTING TO PAINT

Now you are ready to paint. Remember that two or three coats of thin paint are better than one thick coat and that nursery furniture must be well painted to stand up to the constant knocks it will receive. First apply a light coat of paint which has been thinned down with turpentine.

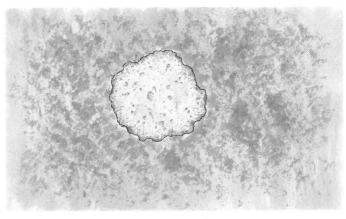

SPONGING

RAGGING

DRAGGING

Don't put too much paint on, and watch out for drips. This first coat may take only 2–3 hours to dry. The second coat need not be thinned with turpentine, but it must be applied sparingly even if this means that a third coat is necessary. This method causes fewer drips and stops the paint from cracking when knocked.

DÉCOUPAGE

Découpage was a popular pastime with Victorian ladies, and involved sticking scraps on to furniture, boxes or screens on a plain-colored background. You can buy replicas of Victorian scraps today; if you cannot find them, cut out bits of wrapping paper or birthday cards. This is a particularly good method of decorating for people who cannot paint. Victorian screens were usually painted black, decorated with nosegays of flowers, angelic children and cherubs, then varnished.

First paint your piece of furniture, either in a plain color or with a ragged, sponged or dragged finish. Carefully cut out your picture, which should preferably be on quite thin paper, using a scalpel knife if the shape is difficult to cut, and stick it down with good glue, making sure that all the edges are firmly stuck. Allow the glue to dry thoroughly, then varnish several times in order to build up a good surface with no obvious rim to the picture. Gloss or medium-sheen varnish is the best. For detailed instructions on making a *découpage* box, see p. 177.

STENCILING

For the American Country or the Scandinavian look, try stenciling a piece of furniture. In the days of the early settlers in America, chair backs were often stenciled with recurring themes such as tulips, doves, unicorns, hearts and the Tree of Life. By the nineteenth century stencil designs had spread throughout settled America, and stenciling had become a popular pastime.

To create an attractive, co-ordinated room, try to paint all the items in the nursery, including boxes and mirrors. But don't tackle everything at once unless you have plenty of time and energy – it is best to progress piece by piece and to stop when you are tired, to avoid rushing and making mistakes. Paint your furniture with eggshell paint, and when it is dry apply the stencil (see p. 56). You can use a stencil kit or you can design one yourself, drawing from traditional American designs such as birds, lyres, pineapples, heads of wheat, acorns and baskets of fruit. Some American designs, particularly those imitating wood grains, became quite wonderfully wild. All sorts of materials from cork ends to rags and sponges can be used to apply the paint.

(a) *All three of these painted chairs are hand-made in English hardwood. From left to right: a child's elbow chair painted directly on to the wood, a red painted high chair, and a two-thirds size farmhouse rocking chair adapted by removing its arms so that it can be used for nursing.*

(b) *A chest decorated by using a combination of sponging techniques and plain painting. The artists adapted an illustration by Henrietta Willebeek-le-Mair to create the enchanting scene on the top.*

(c) *A procession of white geese and fluffy chickens gives a distinctive nursery character to a simple wooden table.*

(d) *Complementary reds and greens brighten this chair and storage chart.*

(e) *Exotic zebras and a matching zebra-striped table that can be used as a surface for reading or drawing.*

(f) *This plain chest of drawers has been stenciled with Swedish-style garlands, making it a charming piece for a little girl's nursery.*

172

PAINTING DIFFERENT TYPES OF FURNITURE

Before decorating any piece of furniture, plan your design roughly on a piece of paper. For inspiration and guidance, take into account the other items in the room, noting the designs and colors of your child's curtains, cushions, play rug and quilt. If you are painting furniture for the nursery of a small baby, don't make your designs too fussy and quaint. Pretty pastel schemes may continue to be appreciated by little girls, but they are likely to be rejected by boys once they reach the age of four or five. If your child is this age, it is worth involving him in your design by preparing rough color sketches and showing them to him, so that you have an advance indication as to whether your scheme will be well received. Take as long

(a) *An old chair from a junk shop, painted all over and decorated with a contentedly sleeping cat. Above the cat is written: 'Pussy cat Pussy cat where have you been?' Nursery rhymes are a good starting point for simple furniture designs like this.*

(b) *A child's beautiful wooden bed and matching mirror, both of them sponged to give a mottled effect. The sleepy fairy motif is repeated at both ends of the bed and on the mirror, and a line from a poem decorates the side.*

(c) *This old stool has been given a new lease of life. The crocodile was painted in acrylics, using spots, crosses and stripes to make the animal as eye-catching as possible.*

(d) *Birds and trees provide the main theme for this unusually painted chair. Pieces such as this will outlast childhood and be treasured for a lifetime. The pale, washed-out colours will also allow the chair to age gracefully.*

(e) *This highly unusual painted crocodile chair stands 13 in high and 5 ft long, allowing two children to sit on it. There is even a place for children to hide their treasures in the crocodile's mouth.*

as you like – remember that one beautifully executed piece of furniture is better than a group which looks messy and amateur.

HEADBOARDS

It is sensible to give your child a headboard, first because he will find it comfortable to lean against when he sits up in bed, and second because it protects the wall from grubby hands and hair. A child's wooden headboard also provides a golden opportunity for you to express yourself in paint – it can be personalized charmingly, either with a simple name or with something more elaborate. Depending on the shape of the headboard, you can paint landscapes or sunny faces, or add small motifs adapted from the curtains or wallpaper.

CHAIRS

You can easily pick up old wooden chairs, either children's ones or school chairs, in junk shops, and transform them into charming pieces that will be treasured for years. Children become very fond of their personalized chairs. There are many professional painters who design infinitely elaborate chairs, but even for the amateur, basic designs are not difficult to execute freehand or using stencils.

CHESTS OF DRAWERS AND WARDROBES

These are more ambitious projects to take on. A built-in closet or free-standing large wardrobe provides plenty of scope for painting a large scene or mural. With a flat-fronted chest of drawers you might paint a large design which cuts right across the lines of the drawers. But in a more traditional room you will achieve a delightful result if you paint or stencil a repeating motif on each drawer and perhaps on the top of the chest.

LEFT: This bedside cupboard and headboard have been dragged and adorned with motifs picked up from the curtain fabric.

BELOW: This highly original picnic table has been decorated with a cake, fruit and cookies, using acrylic paint, then varnished twice. The amusing bear seats are painted to co-ordinate.

RIGHT: This free-standing cabinet has been painted as a house, and can be used either as a dolls' house or as a storage cupboard for toys or clothes.

FAR RIGHT: A chest of drawers and mirror, dragged in a warm yellow and painted with rabbits, flowers and butterflies picked out from the curtain fabric to give a unity to the room.

176

MAKING A DÉCOUPAGE BOX

The art of *découpage* flourished during the Victorian period, and you can make a Victorian-style *découpage* box yourself using the reproduction Victorian scraps that can be purchased at art and craft stores. Alternatively, select cut-outs from old magazines to create a more contemporary *découpage* item. To make a box like the one illustrated here, try to find a plain wooden box in a local junk shop. If the box is varnished or painted, you will have to strip it with paint stripper and sand it down before you start.

MATERIALS
- 1 plain, rectangular wooden box
- Mid-green eggshell paint
- Crackle-glaze (obtainable from craft and paint shops)
- 2 × 1 in/2·5 cm household paintbrushes (one for green paint, one for polyurethane varnish)
- Glue brushes for crackle-glaze
- 5 reproduction Victorian cut-outs
- Spray mount adhesive for gluing down the scraps
- Polyurethane varnish
- Scissors
- Sandpaper

METHOD
1 Wash any dirt or dust off the box so that it is scrupulously clean and dry before you start.
2 Apply 2 coats of mid-green eggshell paint to the outer surfaces of the box, allowing plenty of time for the first coat to dry before applying the second.
3 To achieve an antique, patinated look, apply a coat of crackle-glaze varnish. Leave to dry in a warm, dry place, such as a linen closet or the top of a stove, where the temperature is hot enough for the glaze to crack, but not too hot or it will crack off completely. This box was put in front of an electric fan heater for half an hour at a distance of about 2 feet, and checked at regular intervals.
4 Cut out 5 scraps (1 for the lid of the box and 4 for the sides).
5 Apply glue to the reverse side of each scrap and press them into position, making sure that every piece lies flat. Leave to dry.
6 Apply 4 coats of varnish, allowing each coat to dry thoroughly before the next application.
7 Sand down the varnish lightly to obtain a smooth finish.
8 Apply a final coat of varnish and leave to dry.

Chapter Sixteen

STEPPING OUT

Babies live very close to the floor. What is more, they can make an amazing amount of mess on it. As they get older, children often seem at their happiest sitting and playing on the floor or on floor-level cushions and bean-bags. So think twice before choosing a pastel-colored carpet which will show every stain. You want the floor to be as practical, as comfortable and as safe as possible, as well as looking appealing.

In many ways it is more practical in the early years of regular spillage to avoid carpets and have a harder, cleanable surface like linoleum or tiles. The snag here is that these can look, and even feel, rather cold. However, if you lay attractive rugs in strategic places, especially by the bed, and later add some good-sized cushions and bean-bags, this problem can be overcome. The other advantage of a hard surface is that it is much more suited to games with cars and trains.

The old image of cheap and muddy-colored linoleum dies hard. But nowadays it is sold in many lively colors and patterns and is still very reasonably priced. Vinyl tiles are also hardwearing. Cushioned vinyl is softer.

STAINS AND VARNISHES

You can achieve very attractive effects with stains and varnishes on wooden floors. First, be sure the surface is well sanded to prevent splinters. You can rent an industrial sander for this, or employ a professional to do the work for you. Remember that sanding creates a lot of dust and should be done well before the arrival of a new baby. If the floorboards are in good condition you can simply leave them plain, with a clear varnish, adding rugs for warmth. Varnish also comes in a variety of wood colors which show up the natural grain, such as

Everything in this contemporary nursery is close to floor level, and the rather stark surroundings have been transformed by this marvelous peppermint painted floor. Several coats of varnish seal the paint and ensure a glossy surface. The gray rug, however, provides a warm center.

The designer of this contemporary child's bedroom first painted the floor mid-green, using three coats of emulsion. On the floor she painted lively figures using plastic bottles of children's paint. Then the whole floor was sealed with tough polyurethane varnish.

reddish mahogany or yellowish pine, and in bright greens, blues and yellows. The advantage of using these colored staining varnishes is that they soak into the wood and don't chip off, unlike paint which stays in layers on top. Either varnish a whole floor with the same color or try alternating stripes of different colors or a simple abstract pattern, such as a large circle or triangle in the center of the room with stained borders. It is advisable to add an extra coat of clear varnish over the stain to give complete protection. Use either matte or medium-sheen varnish. Allow at least 48 hours for the stained wood to dry before you apply the clear varnish.

LIMED OR BLEACHED WOOD

This look is particularly appropriate for the Scandinavian style. Before you lime or bleach a floor, you must remove any previous floor surface with a sander and make sure that the floor is scrupulously clean and free of dust. Bleaching a floor is a laborious and difficult process, for which it is best to enlist a professional. To achieve a limed look, divide the room into strips and tackle a strip of approximately four boards at a time. Using white or a dull pastel blue or green eggshell, paint over the boards. Work the paint in with your paintbrush to make certain it is absorbed into the grain. Just before the paint is dry, take a rag and wipe off the excess, rubbing it into the grain again. Experiment at first in a part of the room that won't be too visible. The consistency depends on the type of paint you use, and you may wish to thin it with a little turpentine. Limed wood has a whitened appearance, while bleaching removes the color, making it pale. If you use eggshell you need not varnish. If you use emulsion, then add three coats of varnish.

PAINTED FLOORS

Painting wooden floors can produce some very exciting effects, and also has the advantage of being cheap and hardwearing. A well-painted floor will outlast your child if it is done correctly in the first place. Paint is best used when you wish to hide the wood grain and when you desire a more complicated design or pattern than can be used on a stained floor. If you want to paint your floorboards they must be in good condition and not have gaps down which treasured possessions may slip. If they

Cork floors, though practical, can look rather unexciting. So this one has been cheered up by the addition of a painted road and grass along which children can run their cars. Two colors of cork have been used to create a contrasting border.

are in bad condition you can lay down hardwood and paint on top of that. Hardwood comes in large sheets of 8 ft × 4 ft and can be laid in strips or squares. Be sure the measurements are correct so that there is no discrepancy either way.

Use a household wood primer to prepare the surface if it has not been painted before. After priming the floor, apply two coats of plain paint, using either gloss or eggshell finish. Allow plenty of time for it to dry between coats, and avoid using the paint too thickly.

On the painted floor you can paint an exciting free design, or a more formal pattern worked out beforehand on a grid. A popular idea is to paint a road with bus stops, shops, garage, and so on, along which children can run their toy cars. Old cork floors can also be cheered up with a paint treatment and then varnished.

BORDERS

In a small room, a painted border can be very effective, leaving a separate area in the middle for play, or for a rug. Borders can be stenciled using the spray paint method, as this is a strong paint and will not have to be varnished. They can also be made with potato prints. Cut a square into a half potato and make a simple checker shape, or cut more naturalistic animal designs if you prefer. You can also make a border using the templates that are sold in toy shops. Your older children can help you decide whether to have a pattern of camels or of elephants or dinosaurs

marching round the room. Draw round the templates using a thick felt-tipped pen. Then either leave them as outlines or paint them in.

RUGS

Many of these hard-floor solutions need rugs to warm them up, and these need not be expensive. You can buy imported cotton rugs from India, Portugal and other countries which have wonderfully vivid colors and are easily washable. There are also the charming Numdah rugs from Kashmir, made in soft wool, which come embroidered with many children's themes.

You can make rugs yourself, of course. If you don't want to create your own design, you can easily buy a kit at a craft shop or through one of the many craft magazines available. Cheerful, latch-hooked wool rugs in shapes like the panda and train on p. 183 provide entertainment too. You can also buy kits for needlepoint rugs. With needlepoint you can achieve by far the most intricate and detailed designs, though the rugs will not feel nearly so snug underfoot for children. You can achieve some delightful color combinations with woven rugs. These are particularly appropriate in rooms decorated in Scandinavian style, as there is a long tradition of woven country rugs in Sweden, Norway and Denmark.

Rag rugs, whether prodded or hooked, are coming into fashion, not having been considered at all smart in the past. They are comparatively simple, if time-consuming, to make. Like patchwork, rag rugs developed out of necessity when material to make rugs was scarce and scraps were used instead. They are looped on to a backing of sacking or burlap, and are generally made with scraps of heavy duty woolen fabrics which makes them very soft underfoot. You can create the most charming scenes with animals and flowers or a simple abstract design.

Prodded rugs are made with short pieces of rag. Hooked rugs are a close relation. They are also made from scraps on a burlap backing, but involve hooking long, thin lengths of material rather than short scraps. They originally evolved in Scandinavia and are still particularly popular in America. The burlap backing enables you to use small stitches and therefore achieve a very detailed pattern or picture. Rag rugs are ideal for rooms decorated in English Country or American Country style.

PLAY MATS

When your baby is small and has not yet started to walk, a play mat which you can take around the house with him is extremely useful. The mat will stop your baby from making a dreadful mess on your living-room carpet or wherever you happen to be sitting. You can make one out of cotton lined with 2-oz wadding, or you can use ready-quilted cotton which can easily be machine washed. You can buy lengths of charming quilted fabric with children's designs on them, which are intended for crib covers but are equally good as mats.

CARPETS

If you lay carpet in a baby's room it is bound to get stained. So don't choose an expensive type, and if you already have a good one, cover it with cheap rugs during the early years. Avoid thick pile carpet because it is no good for running toys on. One of the most practical kinds of carpeting for children's rooms is commercial carpeting which is specially made for business use. It is more or less stain-proof and very hardwearing. It comes in plain colors or with small motifs. Most commercial carpets are thin, with very little pile, and do need rugs to brighten them up.

A good way to protect carpets is to use Scotchgard. This gives them a protective finish which means that they resist dirt and spills. Ready-Scotchgarded carpets tend to be a little more expensive to buy, but they do allow you to risk a softer carpet with more pile without worrying about stains. You might consider having a really cheap carpet or bare boards for the first few years, until the child is potty-trained and fewer accidents are likely to happen, and choose a more expensive Scotchgarded carpet later.

When deciding on your carpet color, remember that a bright clear color gives a room a real lift and tends to make it appear lighter. A clear color is often better than neutrals and browns. While a large swirling pattern is rather overpowering for a small child, carpets with a small fleck pattern conceal the dirt and stains better than absolutely plain ones. If there is a particular place in the nursery where there are likely to be regular spills, perhaps around a table where the children paint or eat, you could protect that bit of the carpet by covering it with some plastic or perhaps a piece of cut-out linoleum.

(a) *and* (b) *Thick-pile woolen latch-hooked rugs* (c) *A light cotton appliqué play mat* (d) *A Victorian-style tapestry rug* (e) *A hand-hooked rag rug*

a

b

c

d

e

183

MAKING A RAG RUG

There are several different methods of making rag rugs, but the simplest technique and the one used in working traditional rugs is the hand-hooked method. The charming "cow" rug here is made by this method and is based on a child's drawing, but any bold, colorful design would do just as well.

MATERIALS
Because this type of rug is by definition a "one off" item, it is not possible to give precise quantities or measurements. However, you will need the following materials.
- Graph paper for marking out your design. (You can, however, draw the design directly on to the backing fabric with an indelible crayon.)
- Backing: any even, firmly woven fabric with a large weave.
- Yarn: wool strips in a variety of textures were used here, but you could use any strips of cloth of a similar type/weight. (Note: pre-washed cloth is less likely to fray or unravel.)

- Frame: this is optional, but it does ensure even hooking and stops the rug from getting a "waistline." Frames are available in various sizes or can be homemade (see diagram i). Stretch the backing fabric tightly over the frame and secure it with strong thumbtacks. Ensure that the frame is the right size for your project: the finished article can be longer than the frame because it can be rolled around one of the stretchers, but it cannot be wider.
- Hook: a special tool, very similar to a crochet hook, can be purchased from craft stores.
- Rug binding or tape (for finishing off raw edges).
- Lining: heavy burlap or any strong, closely woven fabric, cut 1½in/4cm larger all around than the rug. The lining is optional, but it does save wear and help to keep the rug in shape. Alternatively, a latex backing can be applied to the back of an unlined rug to make it slip-proof and to help anchor the stitches.

MAKING UP
1 To make the "yarn," cut the strips of fabric along the grain of the material and as long as possible – cutting on the bias will cause bad fraying. The width of the strips depends on the weight of the fabric used, the type of backing and the effect you want to create. As a rule the heavier the fabric, the thinner the strip can be. If you need to join strips together, cut the ends diagonally and stitch across the top of the diagonal (see diagram ii). Trim the seam and press open.
2 Draw the design on graph paper or draw directly on the backing fabric.
3 Hooking:
(a) Hold a strip of fabric firmly beneath the backing

material on the reverse side. From the right side of the fabric, push the hook through (see diagram iii), hook around the strip and pull it through the backing to form a loop on the right side (see diagram iv). (b) Continue to hook through loops, making sure that they are evenly spaced and regular in height (see diagram v), but not too short. Larger loops make a more durable carpet.

(c) To finish a length of yarn, pull the ends up to the top. These can be cut down later to lie lower than the pile of the rest of the rug.

4 To make the "cow" rug, first hook the cow design, followed by the border. For the background color, hook around the outlines of the cow and the border and then fill in the background. To create a more interesting texture, try varying the background color and changing the direction of the hooking.

5 If the backing fabric finishes with a raw edge, it is a good idea to bind this to prevent fraying. Using strong thread, sew the rug binding or tape on the right side of the backing close to the edge of the rug stitches. Cut off the excess backing to within about $\frac{2}{3}$ in/2 cm on each side, fold the edges to the back and sew the binding to the back of the rug, making sure that the stitches do not show through to the right side. (Binding is unnecessary if you decide to line the rug – see (**6**) below.)

6 To line your rug, cut out a piece of cloth following the instructions above. Turn back the edges of unworked backing fabric to form a hem. Making sure that the grain of the backing and that of the lining are aligned, pin the lining at intervals to the back of the rug, from the center outwards. Sew the lining to the hem of the rug about $\frac{5}{8}$ in/1.5 cm from the edge on each side, using strong thread and herringbone stitch.

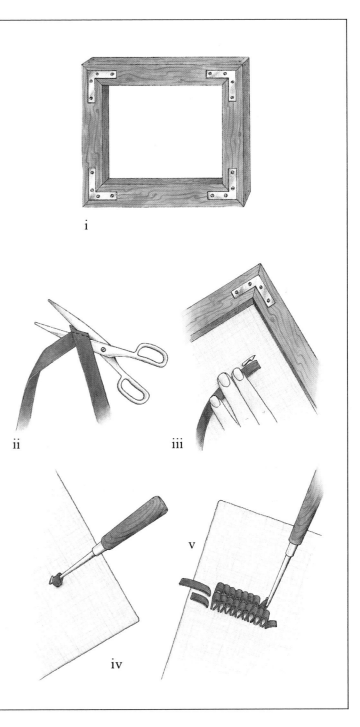

i

ii

iii

iv

v

ARTISTS, SHOPS AND SUPPLIERS

For references to illustrations in the text showing products and designs contributed by these companies, please consult the picture credits on page 189.

NAME/ADDRESS	PRODUCTS/SERVICES
Deirdre Amsden Studio 38A Colmans Court 45 Morris Road London E14 6NQ England (Tel: 01-987 9569)	One-off designs for patchwork quilts and hangings; commissions undertaken, time permitting. Worldwide orders taken.
Laura Ashley 1300 MacArthur Blvd. Mahwah NJ 07430 (Tel: 201-934 3000)	Garments for women and children + wide range of furnishing fabrics, wallpapers and accessories. Branches nationwide.
Beaudesert Charlotte Moss 131 East 70th Street New York NY 10021 (Tel: 212 722 3320) Trilogy Village Green PO Box 640 Bedford New York NY 10506 (Tel: 914 234 3021)	Furnishing fabrics; interior design and decorating service.
Elizabeth Bradley Designs 1 West End Beaumaris Anglesey North Wales LL58 8BD (Tel: 0248-811055)	Victorian tapestry cushion and rug kits. Worldwide mail order service.

NAME/ADDRESS	PRODUCTS/SERVICES
Debbie Booth English Willow Basket Makers Elmham Road Beetley Dereham Norfolk NR20 4BW England (Tel: 0362-860918)	Traditional willow baskets, from cradles to hampers, log baskets to eel traps; customers' own designs made to order. Worldwide orders taken.
Bundles 224 Century Building Brunswick Dock Liverpool L3 4AA England (Tel: 051-709 5595)	Designer wallpapers, fabrics, borders and hand-painted furniture to order. Worldwide orders taken.
Rohays Butter 48 Brunswick Gardens London W8 4AN England (Tel: 01 229 3239)	Hand-painted furniture, cut-outs, lampshades, murals, tiles and blinds. Worldwide orders taken.
Chancery Marketing Ltd Schmid 55 Pacella Park Drive Randolph Massachusetts 02368 (Tel: 617 961 3000)	Beatrix Potter musical figurines, hanging ornaments, photo frames, night-lights and musical water-balls. Schmid: showrooms in Atlanta, Denver, Minneapolis, Bedford, Detroit, New York, Chicago, Kansas, San Francisco, Columbus, Los Angeles, Seattle, Dallas. *(contd)*

NAME/ADDRESS	PRODUCTS/SERVICES
CANADIAN DISTRIBUTORS: Samaco Trading Ltd 55E East Beavercreek Road Richmond Hill Ontario Canada L4B 1E8 (Tel: 416 731 3232)	
The Conran Shop Michelin House 81 Fulham Road London SW3 6RD England (Tel: 01–589 7401)	Retailers of a large range of items, both practical and decorative, to furnish/accessorize the home. Worldwide orders taken.
Descamps Ltd Boutique Descamps 723 Madison Avenue New York, NY 10121	Descamps offer a delightful range of bedlinen and accessories (change bags, cot sets, etc.) for babies and infants – available from the boutique on Madison Ave, by mail order from same address, and selected stores nationwide. Other main US stockists in: Dallas, Los Angeles, Miami and Philadelphia.

NAME/ADDRESS	PRODUCTS/SERVICES
Designers Guild Osborne and Little Suite 1503N – 15th Floor 979 Third Avenue New York NY 10022 (Tel: 212 751 3333)	Interior design, furnishing fabrics and wallpapers. Any UK lines unavailable in US can be obtained via UK showroom.
Dragons of Walton Street Ltd 23 Walton Street, London SW3 2HX England (Tel: 01-589 3795)	Hand-painted furniture; interior design service. Worldwide orders taken.
Heal's Marketing Design 444 Lafayette Street New York NY 10003 (Tel: 212-777-8080)	All items to furnish the home – both practical and decorative.
Ruth Hydes Textiles (Cheshire) 7 Artlebrook Cottages Audlem Road Hatherton Nantwich Cheshire CW5 7QT England (Tel: 0270-841836)	Designer/maker of fine appliqué shades, cushions and pictures in hand-dyed cotton. Worldwide mail order service available.
Jameson Designs 29 Elystan Street London SW3 3NT (Tel: 01-584 7642)	Architects and interior designers dealing with residential and commercial projects in UK and abroad.
Karl's Painted Swedish Furniture The Syllian Collections 21 East 67th Street New York NY 10021 (Tel: 212 988 7930)	Exclusively designed Swedish period furniture, wallpapers, borders, fabrics and co-ordinated accessories.
Monogrammed Linen Shop 168 Walton Street London SW3 2JL England (Tel: 01-589 4033)	Continental and British bedlinen, towels (monogrammed to order), traditional childrenswear, gifts. Worldwide mail order service. All credit cards and telephone orders accepted.
Anthea Moore Ede 16 Victoria Grove London W8 5RW England (Tel: 0579-42336)	Traditional babies' and children's clothes (0–14 years). Worldwide orders taken.
Katie Morgan Sudeley Castle Craft Workshops Winchcombe Gloucestershire England (Tel: 0242-604233)	Decorative painting, screens, firescreens and fairground art to order. Worldwide orders taken.
Helen Napper c/o Anne Thomson Sue Rankin Gallery 670 Fulham Road London SW6 5RX England (Tel: 01-736 4120)	One-off paintings on all kinds of furniture and interiors, to commission.
Naturally British British Handmade Crafts 13 New Row London WC2 4LF England (Tel: 01-240 0551)	Christening presents and toys – all British made. Worldwide mail and credit card orders taken.
The Nursery Window Cowtan & Tout Inc. 979 3rd Avenue New York NY 10022 (Tel: 212 753 4488)	Suppliers of children's wallpapers, fabrics and accessories.
Osborne and Little 65 Commerce Road Stamford CT 06902 (Tel: 203–359–1500)	Leading English designers of fabrics and wallpapers, noted for wide range of original patterns in imaginative colorings.
Pallu and Lake London Interior Designers Centre 1 Cringle Street London SW8 5BX England	Distributor of furnishing fabrics, wallpapers and furniture, sold through interior decorators and designers plus specialist retailers, e.g. The Charles Hammond Shop, 253 Fulham Road, London SW3, England, which offers worldwide mail order service.
Paper Moon Collings and Aikman 23645 Mercantile Road Cleveland Ohio 44122 (Tel: 216 464 3700)	Distributors of wallpapers, borders and co-ordinating fabrics.
Rainbow Designs Eden Toys 112 West 34th Street New York NY 10120 (Tel: 212 564 5980)	Manufacturers and distributors of licensed Beatrix Potter products to good gift and toyshops.
Royal Doulton Ltd Royal Doulton USA Inc. 700 Cottontail Lane Somerset New Jersey 08873 (Tel: 201 356 7880)	Gift-boxed, fine china nursery ware for use at meal times, plus figures, lamps and decorative items to collect.
Arthur Sanderson & Son Ltd Suite 403 The 979 Building 3rd Avenue New York NY 10022 (Tel: 212-319-7220)	Distributor and very extensive range of wallpapers, fabrics, paints and carpets. Showroom also retails furniture. Fabric, etc., distributed internationally. Otherwise only available in US through interior designers and decorators.
Shyam Ahuja 201 East 56th Street 3rd Avenue New York NY 10022 (Tel: 212 644 5910)	Suppliers of rugs, fabrics and furnishing accessories. US: available throughout Macey's stores in California – San Francisco, San Mateo and Sacramento
Simplantex (Eastbourne) Ltd and Première Baby Miss Tara Lutton Perry Enterprises Ltd 113 W. Weber Drive Muncie Indiana 47303 (Tel: 317 284 2226)	Complete range of nursery bedding and accessories + soft toy distribution.
The Singing Tree 69 New Kings Road London SW6 4SQ England (Tel: 01-736 4527)	A leading specialist in dolls' houses, supplying all miniature accessories – any item can be made to order. Orders taken worldwide. Catalogue available.
Annie Sloan Knutsford House Park Street Bladon Oxford OX7 1RW England (Tel: 0993-812590)	Painted furniture and murals; supplier of decorative paint brushes and glazes; courses in decorative painting.
Souleiado Pierre Deux 369/381 Bleecker Street New York NY 10014 (Tel: 212 243 7740 (No. 369) and 212 675 4054 (No. 381)) Pierre Deux 870 Madison Avenue New York NY 10021 (Tel: 212 570 9343)	French provençal printed fabrics. Other locations for Pierre Deux shops: Atlanta, Bal Harbor, Beverly Hills, Boston, Carmel, Chicago, Dallas, Houston, Kansas City, New Orleans, Palm Beach, San Francisco, Scottsdale, Seattle, Washington.
Timney Fowler Ltd Christopher Hyland Inc Suite 1708 D & D Building 979 3rd Avenue New York NY 10022 (Tel: 212 688 6121)	Mainly black and white neo-classical prints – wallpapers, fabrics, ceramics.

NAME/ADDRESS	PRODUCTS/SERVICES
Tissunique Ltd Classic Revivals 1 Design Centre Place Suite 545 Boston Mass 02210 (Tel: 617 574 9030)	Unique range of furnishing fabrics, wallpapers, and borders. Selection of silks, damasks and trimmings. Cuttings provided + advice where to buy.
Upstairs Shop Don Gleeson Summer Hill Ltd 2682H Middle Field Road Redwood City CA 94063 (Tel: 415 363 2600)	An exclusive range of fabrics, wallpapers and soft furnishings for the bedroom. Twelve showrooms throughout the US.

NAME/ADDRESS	PRODUCTS/SERVICES
Carolyn Warrender Stencil Designs Ltd 91 Lower Sloane Street London SW1 W8DA England (Tel: 01-730 0728)	Retailers of extensive range of pre-cut stencils, stencil accessories and equipment for making/cutting stencils. Complete custom stencilling service; mail order service catalogue. £1.35 (incl. p+p).
Anne Wilkinson Designs Ltd Unit 3 Saxon Way Battledown Industrial Estate Cheltenham Gloucestershire GL52 6QX England (Tel: 0242-578666)	Wholesaler for screen-printed nursery fabric and items, including Winnie the Pooh, Beatrix Potter animals and other children's book characters. Products retailed throughout UK and US. Mail orders taken.

NAME/ADDRESS	PRODUCTS/SERVICES
Peter de Wit 21 Greenwich Church Street Greenwich London SE10 9BJ England (Tel: 01-305 0048)	Toymaker, painted furniture and decorative artist. Worldwide mail order service.

We realize that this list of contributors to the book is by no means comprehensive and apologize for any unintentional omissions.

PICTURE ACKNOWLEDGEMENTS

_____

For loan of items for the special photography by Graham Challifour, Graham Miller and Peter Rauter the authors and publishers wish to extend their grateful thanks to the following:

Moyra Bannister, Felicity Binyon, Elizabeth Bradley Designs, Wendy Collin and Julia Finzel, Lady Daphne Bailey, English Willow Baskets, Anca Groves, Hippo Hall, Tessa Howes, Sarah Jones, Sarah Kirtin, Susan Luxton for Maggie Interiors, The Monogrammed Linen Shop, Helen Napper, Naturally British, Neal Street East, The Nursery Window, Graham Piggott, Simplantex, Teddy Bears, Tissunique, Peter de Wit Toys.

INDEX

Figures in *italics* refer to captions.

Down a Garden Path
To Places of Love and Joy

by

KARLA DORNACHER

4

To Michael, Michelle, Gary, and Alexis for being the best family this wife, mom, and grandma could ever have hoped for!

To Kathy Glass & Peggy Beardsley, my garden friends, for expressing God's love to me through your prayers, encouragements, and words of wisdom.

To Sandi Phillips, my dear friend and mentor, for letting me see "Christ in you" and believing in the "Christ in me."

To Jack Countryman, my publisher, for believing in me and giving me the opportunity to share my heart and my vision.

To Jesus, the Master Gardener of my life, for pouring His life and love into my heart and causing flowers to grow where there were once only weeds.

To Jack's wife and my good friend, Marsha, for sharing your delightful enthusiasm for life and your cheerful words of encouragement.

To all those at J. Countryman for giving of yourselves to the work of "touching lives and changing lives."

To Terri Gibbs, my editor, for removing the rocks and pulling out the weeds of my writing to enable this book to bear more fruit.

To Mark and Vicki Romig, my friends, for their watercolor wisdom, and especially to Vicki for running to my aide whenever I cried "help!"

Welcome friend

Whether you are an avid gardener, a casual cultivator, or one who simply enjoys the beauty and bounty of a garden well-tended, I invite you to stroll with me along the fragrant path of this special garden. Together we will delight in its beauty, discover some of its secrets, and even share in its bountiful harvest.

From the first pages of the Bible through to the last, we find God portrayed as the Master Gardener. It is my hope that through the stories and illustrations of this small book He will be revealed to you in a new way.

So please join me as we follow the path of the Master Gardener. Walk slowly, listen carefully, and you will surely hear His voice.

Your friend,
Karla

8

The Lord God planted a garden

GENESIS 2:8

I saw an ad in the paper for a class
on how to become a "master gardener."
I love to garden, but if you came to visit my garden
you would find that I am much more of a dabbler than a "master"!

In fact, God is the only *true* Master Gardener.

He not only created the first garden,
He also created you and the spiritual "garden of your heart."
His desire is for you to be
a strong, healthy, well-watered garden —
even in the midst of the "weeds, thistles, and thorns" of daily life.
He longs for you to be firmly rooted and established
in His love and to be able to recognize the touch of His hand
as He labors in the spiritual garden of your life:
tilling , planting , watering , and weeding .

Is there an area of your life that needs the special touch
of the Master's hand? Call to Him today.
Ask Him to make a beautiful, bountiful garden of your life
for it is His pleasure and delight
to watch you grow , blossom , and bear much fruit !

Let the whole

with

Psalm 72:19

12

earth be filled

His glory

MORNING

GLORY

Heavenly Seed Co.

13

There are many "gates" along life's way that open to fields
of thorny thistles, tangled weeds, and briar woods.
But there is only one gate
that opens into the presence of the Master Gardener —
and Jesus is that Gate!

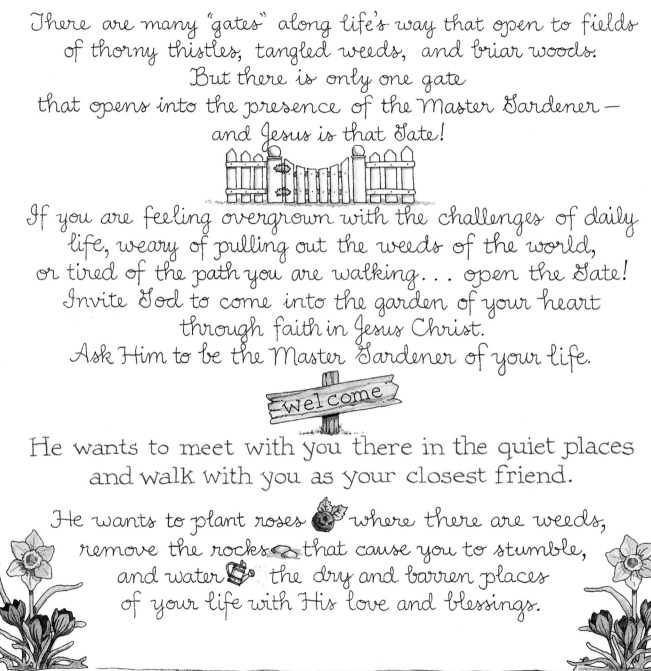

If you are feeling overgrown with the challenges of daily
life, weary of pulling out the weeds of the world,
or tired of the path you are walking . . . open the Gate!
Invite God to come into the garden of your heart
through faith in Jesus Christ.
Ask Him to be the Master Gardener of your life.

He wants to meet with you there in the quiet places
and walk with you as your closest friend.

He wants to plant roses where there are weeds,
remove the rocks that cause you to stumble,
and water the dry and barren places
of your life with His love and blessings.

Enter His gates with thanksgiving

welcome

Psalm 100:4

15

We are
to God
the fragrance
of Christ

2 Corinthians 2:15

Fragrant Prayer Potpourri

Choose any and all of these ingredients,
for they compliment each other well.
Simply mix together with an abundance of love and faith —
anytime, night or day.

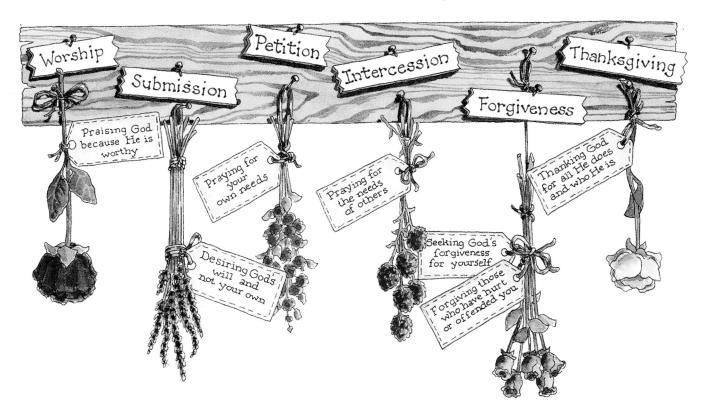

Worship — Praising God because He is worthy

Submission — Desiring Gods will and not your own

Petition — Praying for your own needs

Intercession — Praying for the needs of others

Forgiveness — Seeking God's forgiveness for yourself / Forgiving those who have hurt or offended you

Thanksgiving — Thanking God for all He does and who He is

Beautiful blooms and a bountiful harvest
require good soil.

In the Bible, Jesus uses a word picture of garden dirt
to help us understand how the beauty and the bounty
of our character, our life, and our deeds
are dependent upon the condition of our heart·soil.
The seed of God's Word requires good soil to germinate,
take root, grow deep, and bear abundant fruit.

Good heart·soil is an ongoing, never-ending process.
As you open your heart
to the tender hand of the Master Gardener,
He is able to till the hard places,
remove the rocks, and pull up the weeds of the world
that would entangle and choke out the life of His love.

Take time to cultivate your relationship
with the Master Gardener. Ask Him to show you any areas
of your heart·soil where you need to let go and let Him work.
Seek to be the beautiful and bountiful
garden He designed you to be.

Search me O God, and know my heart,

Pure in Heart

...venly Seed Co

...Psalm 139:23

Jesus, I want the garden of my life
to be as beautiful and as bountiful as You.

20

Weeds to Clean Out
- ☐ WORRY
- ☐ PRIDE
- ☐ JEALOUSY
- ☐ BUSYNESS
- ☐ FEAR
- ☐ COMPLACENCY
- ☐ GREED
- ☐ ANGER
- ☐ SELF-PITY
- ☐ GOSSIP
- ☐ BUSYBODY
- ☐ LUST
- ☐ LAZYNESS

Create in me
a rich and fertile heart soil, O God,
and clean out every weed that
keeps me from enjoying Your presence
and bringing You glory.

21

There are vegetable gardens and perennial gardens,
gardens to attract butterflies, and some designed for their perfume.
As you pour over the seed catalogs and garden books,
you must ask yourself what is the purpose of your garden.
What do you want to reap from your garden plot?
This will determine the seed that you sow. You can then choose the
perfect seeds to produce the bounty you desire.

The Bible is the book of inspiration for gardeners of the heart.
There you will come to know and love
the Master Gardener and delight in His wisdom.
Its pages are filled with seeds of promise and hope.
As you open your heart ♥, He will plant in you
the perfect seeds to produce a rich and fulfilling garden-life.
And while you are there you will also be inspired
by stories of other gardeners
who planted seeds of faith and patience
and reaped abundant harvests of God's grace and goodness.

As God's Word takes root and grows in your heart
it will naturally begin to blossom and bear fruit.
It is through the fruit of your words, attitudes, and deeds
that you become a partner with the Master Gardener,
scattering the seeds of His love in the lives of others.

Sow. Faith;
reap
blessing

23

He who sows bountifully

24

God loves a
cheerful
giver.
2 CORINTHIANS 9:7

Charity
Chutney
V. W. M. S.

Good
Deed

Peachy
Praise

Prayer
Preserves

Sweet
Words

will also reap bountifully.

2 Corinthians 9:6

25

The Lord's love surrounds those who trust Him.

Psalm 32:10NC

Love grows here

26

One summer, while living in Alaska, we tilled a small plot
of ground for a vegetable garden. More than one
well-meaning neighbor stopped by to muse over the fact
that we had no fence around our garden and in Alaska,
that most likely meant "free lunch" for a visiting moose.

However, my enthusiasm for gardening and a lack of funds led
me to trust God to be the "fence of protection"
around our garden. Much to the amazement
of our neighbors, we found mooseprints in the garden twice
and chased out one lost cow, but nothing was eaten!
One spinach plant had been stepped on and even it lived!!

Love grows here

Your life is of far greater value than a small patch of dirt
and a few peas or cauliflowers!
You don't need to be afraid
of the "predators or pests" of life —
those circumstances that try to discourage you
and eat away at your peace of mind.
God has promised to be your protection.
His strong outstretched arms will keep you safe.

I will trust in the shelter of your wings

I will trust in the shelter of your wings

I will trust in the shelter of your wings

I will trust in the shelter of your wings

God has promised
to be your hiding place,
your refuge
when you seek protection,
and a safe haven
when you need to retreat.

Under the shadow of His wings
nothing can harm you.

As we were cleaning the brush for our garden in Alaska,
I knew this would be my most challenging garden ever.
In addition to the short growing season,
we had no water on our property. I would have to haul
the water in by barrels and hand water each plant individually.
I worked the soil beneath each plant and built up a reservoir around
it so not a drop of water would be lost.
Each thirsty plant from seedtime to harvest,
received my undivided attention as I poured out
life-giving water upon it's roots and tended to it's needs.

Every garden requires water to give life to the seed,
develop a deep root system, grow strong, and bear fruit.
Without water a garden dies.

Are you thirsty? Is your garden wilted and weak?
Is your heart-soil dry and parched?
Jesus says "Come to Me, I will water you with living water".
The Master Gardener calls you by name.
Go to Him and tell Him your need.
Spend time with Him and feel the touch of His tender mercy.
Pray and ask Him to water you deeply with His presence.
Let your roots soak up His life-giving love. Don't waste a drop,
and your soul will be like a well-watered garden.

Your soul
shall be
like a
well~
watered
garden.

Jeremiah 31:12

May your roots go down deep into the soil of God's marvelous love...

Ephesians 3:17 TLB

Star-of-Bethlehem.

32

Lord,
may the roots of my heart —
my thoughts, my desires, my words,
and my deeds — be firmly established
in the soil of your wonderful love.
Help me today and every day,
to draw my nourishment
from You and Your Word.

And Lord, during the dry times,
give me the strength to keep growing deeper,
seeking You always.

Amen

There is a story in the Bible about a vine and its branches. It tells us that Jesus is the true Vine and we, as believers, are His branches. We are part of Him and He is part of us, joined together as one.

Each branch receives its life through the Vine. As you spend time with Jesus — reading your Bible and letting Him speak to your heart - - His life will flow in and through you, bringing fruitfulness and fulfillment.

But there is one major difference between God's grapevine and those here on earth. As branches of the true Vine we have been given a will ~ we must choose either to meet with Him each day and enjoy the benefits of His love and wisdom or ignore Him and try to face the challenges of life in our own limited strength.

Are you wilting from the cares of the world? Do you feel dry and empty? Choose to set aside time to be with Jesus today and every day. Enjoy the life that is yours in Him!

I am the vine; you are the branches... abide in Me...

John 15:5

Just for you . . .

you will be like a tree planted by streams of wa[ter]...[l]uscious fruit in season, and your leaves will not die.

As our roots grow deep in God's love, He produces fruit in our lives such as a peaceful heart, joy, and the desire to help others. Use this space to thank God for the fruit He is producing in your life.

When we hung our first bird feeder on the fence, I didn't stop to consider that the birds would help me plant the flowerbeds below. I had carefully planted these beds myself in a soft pallette of whites, pinks, and purples. So I cringed when I saw the little sunflower seedlings popping up everywhere! Though uninvited, I did not have the heart to pull them out. Later, I was so glad I had let them grow, for they added a wonderful whimsy to our garden.

As they grew, they seemed to be reaching with outstretched arms to the heavens.

Their cheerful faces greeted the morning sun with a smile, and their uplifted heads followed its path of light throughout the day.

Oh, that we would do the same. Let's greet the Son in the morning with a smile and keep our eyes focused on Him every moment of the day.

The Lord bless you and keep you; the Lord make His face shine upon you . . . .

Numbers 6:24,25

39

Forget not all

Forget-Me-Not

Seeds of Praise

Psalm 103:2

His benefits

What are some of the benefits of knowing God that you don't want to forget?

Be still and know that I am God

Sometimes my life is so busy the only thing
I am able to do in my garden is work.
The tasks I normally enjoy become chores and worst of all,
I do not take the time to simply
rest and delight in the garden's beauty.

There is a time for tilling , a time for planting,
a time for weeding, and a time for resting.
Jesus calls to us in the midst of our busyness.
He invites us to spend time with Him.

Take time to be still. Lay aside your tools,
your seed packets, your garden gloves, and sit with Him.
Delight in His beauty and the glory of His creation.

Look into His Word and see the depth of His love for you.
Be refreshed with His peace
and strengthened by His promises.
Let Him restore to you the joy of the simple tasks of life.

As you leave your quiet place, the world will know
you have been in the presence of the Master Gardener.

Your promises are sweeter than

sweet to me,

honey in my mouth!

PSALM 119:103 NIV

45

Butterflies are delightful reminders
of the power of God's love to transform our lives.
Watching a butterfly dance in the air,
it is hard to believe that it was once a common caterpillar.
Within the protective covering of the chrysalis,
the lowly, earthbound caterpillar is slowly transformed
into a remarkable creature of freedom and beauty.

A similar process of transformation takes place in our lives
as we allow God's Holy Spirit to soften our hearts
and change our pattern of thinking. Only God's love
and truth can bring genuine freedom and beauty
into our lives by changing us from the inside out.

As you live in obedience to God's Word each day,
your life will be transformed ~
you will become more and more like Jesus.

If anyone
is in
Christ,

he is
a new
creation

2 CORINTHIANS 5:17

47

Oh, sing to the Lord a new song!

God lives here

Home Sweet Home
PSALM 98:1

48

Rejoice, and sing!

Write the words to a favorite song of praise,
and sing it to God today!

Though the garden plot
appears to be barren and bleak,
winter is a necessary season of
rest and regeneration.
In the cold stillness the Master Gardener
is at work, revealing His design and
purpose for your life.

This is a time, not only of reflecting on
the past, but also of looking forward,
with expectation, to what lies ahead.
Winter always gives way to spring.

Buds bursting with promise,
the song of the sparrow
as it builds its nest,
the freshly tilled soil ready for seed—
these signs of spring bring
a joyful celebration of new life.

The Master Gardener
specializes in new beginnings!
He sows His seeds of mercy
new every morning
in the garden of your heart.
This is a season of rejoicing!

Summer is the most fun season of life,
as well as the most work!
The garden is filled with the beauty of
flowers in full bloom,
the celebration of friendships,
and the laughter of life!
It is also the time of weeding,
battling garden pests and disease,
fertilizing, and watering.

Be careful during this season to stop
and pick a bouquet of God's goodness
in the midst of your busy day!

As the summer sun yields to the harvest
moon and the bright summer colors
give way to the beauty of autumn leaves,
let your heart be filled with thanksgiving.

Fall is the time for reaping the rewards
of your labor of faith,
the abundance of God's provision.
It is the season for storing
within your heart the memories
of all He has done for you...
memories to carry with you
through the cold days of winter.

51

Let the peace of God

Seeds of Peace

Heavenly Seed Co.

Colossians 3:15

rule in your hearts.

Blessed
are the
peacemakers

GOD SHALL SUPPLY
ALL YOUR NEEDS

The birds of our neighborhood know we love them.
We enjoy them so much that we have filled our garden
with birdhouses 🏠 , birdbaths 🏺 , and feeders.
God loves these little birds more then we do.
They belong to Him. He cares for them long after
our feeder is empty or the birdbath dries up.

The birds don't worry about their needs;
they trust in God's provision
and give thanks with a joyful song!
God doesn't want you to worry about
your needs either — your clothes, house, or food.

Your heavenly Father loves you.
You are more valuable to Him than many sparrows.
He has promised that if you will seek Him first —
get to know Him, trust Him, and walk in His ways —
He will always supply what is needed in your life.

What are you trusting the Lord for today?

Date:

Remember, He will direct your paths.

Trust in the Lord with all your heart, and lean not on your own understanding; in all your ways acknowledge Him, and He shall direct your paths.

PROVERBS 3:5,6

THIS WAY

REST
REFRESHING

RETREAT
BLESSING
JOY

The path of salvation is a narrow one,
but not so narrow that you must walk it alone.
It is the perfect width for the Master Gardener
to walk beside you as your Father and your Friend.

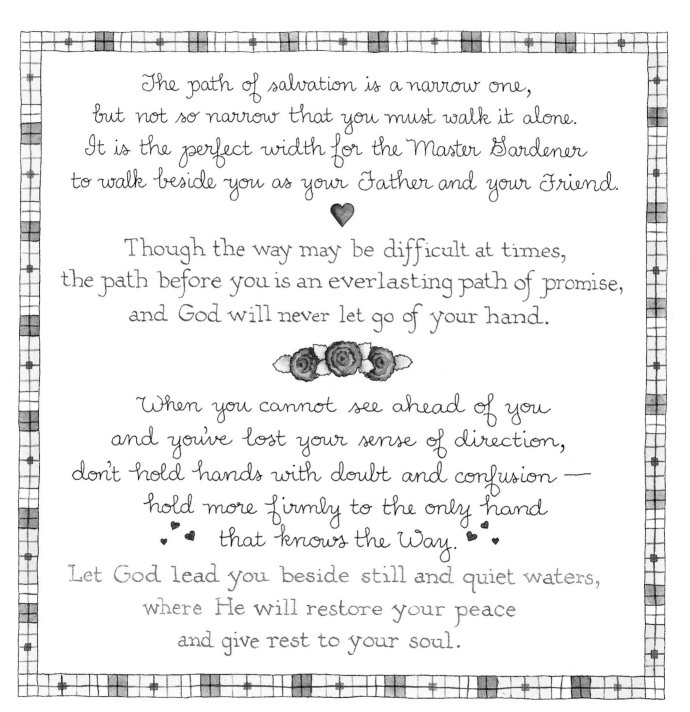

Though the way may be difficult at times,
the path before you is an everlasting path of promise,
and God will never let go of your hand.

When you cannot see ahead of you
and you've lost your sense of direction,
don't hold hands with doubt and confusion —
hold more firmly to the only hand
that knows the Way.
Let God lead you beside still and quiet waters,
where He will restore your peace
and give rest to your soul.

He leads me beside quiet waters

Psalm 23:2 NIV

59

In the time of trouble He shall hide me in His Pavilion.

Psalm 27:5

Welcome

60

No one is exempt from times of trouble.
But as you face the storms of life, you can always
stand confident that Jesus wants you to come to Him.
He wants to shelter you in the pavilion of His tender care.

There are not two chairs in this pavilion,
but a loveseat  where Jesus wants to sit with you
and embrace you with the strength of His love and protection.
When you come into His presence
and share your deepest burdens with Him,
He will lift them from you and give you rest and peace.

The Holy Spirit, shown here as a dove,
comes to bring comfort, encouragement, and hope.

Let this pavilion be a place
to draw away with  God, to worship  Him,
to hear His voice,
to trust Him as your best friend.

I come to the garden alone
while the dew is still on the roses . . .

And He walks with me,

And He tells me I am

And the joy we

None other

and He talks with me,

His own;

share as we tarry there,

has ever known.

from the song In the Garden by Charles Austin Miles, 1913

63

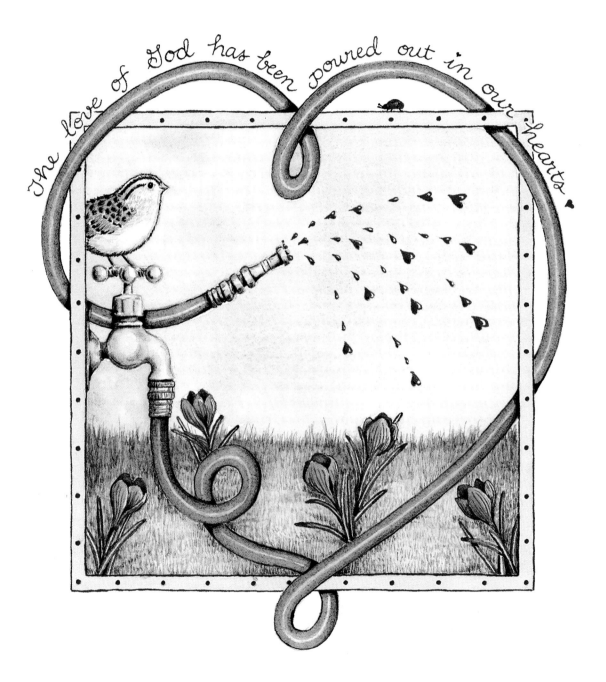

The love of God has been poured out in our hearts.

What are some of the blessings of love that God has poured out in your life?

COME, LET US REJOICE

My garden was in all it's glory — full bloom, neat, and tidy.
We covered the tables with lace tablecloths
and quilts and placed a fresh bouquet on each one.
With colorful ribbons, I tied pansies and sprigs of ivy
to the hand-lettered placecards.
As the women arrived, with garden hats and gifts,
the air was filled with the joyful sounds of love and laughter.
We were rejoicing in the birth of a baby!
We were celebrating life!

God's Word encourages us to celebrate all the wonderful things
He has done for us . . . even the everyday things like friendship,
a beautiful sunset, or a job well done.

What good thing has God done for you?
Or for someone you know?
You don't have to wait for a birthday or anniversary to celebrate.
And you don't need to have lace or quilts or gifts.
You can pull out the barbecue, have a potluck,
or just do a dessert.
The important thing is to celebrate!

Show me Your ways,

teach me

lead me in Your

This is the Way

Dead End

Life Everlasting

O LORD,

Your paths;

truth and teach me.

Walk by faith,

not by sight

2 CORINTHIANS 5:7

So we,
being many,
are one body
in Christ.

Romans 12:5

Every flower has its own personality ~
a uniquely beautiful shape, color, and texture.
When you gather these "personalities" together and arrange them in
a bouquet, they create a wonderful harmony of beauty and fragrance.

God created you just as beautiful and unique as any flower.
There is no one else like you. He has designed you
with a unique combination of gifts and talents, strengths
and life experiences. But He never designed you to stand alone.
You are an important and valuable "flower" in His bouquet.

When you allow the Master Gardener
to take the single "stem" of your life and place it in the beautiful
bouquet of the Body of Christ, something extraordinary
happens. God's church needs the shape, color, and texture that only
you can give. Perhaps you fit best in the nursery or in a Sunday
school class or in the choir. Perhaps you enjoy cooking meals for
those in need or ministering in prayer.

As you come together with other believers in worship and service,
God creates a fragrance of love and kindness
that can be poured out abundantly on the world!

He who sows righteousness

LOVE
Heavenly Seed Co

PRAYER
Kingdom Seeds

FAITH
God's Good Seed

TRUTH
Heavenly Seed Co

MIX
GOOD DEEDS
KINGDOM SEEDS

...reaps a sure reward

Proverbs 11:18 NIV

A few years ago a forget-me-not, with its tiny blue flowers, appeared amidst my deep pink azalea border. I had not planted this little charmer, but I greeted it as a gift from God ~ delivered most likely by one of my flying friends.

Every year the forget-me-not has multiplied and even though I never considered planting these two together, the harmony they create today is breathtaking!
I delight to confess to all who compliment me on its beauty that this striking combination is God's design, not mine!

God also has a special design for each of our lives.
Sometimes He allows "seeds" of circumstance or relationships to take root that we would never have chosen for ourselves. But He knows what is best for us.
And though we may not be able to see its beauty or purpose today, we can be confident that whatever God allows in our lives will be for our good, to help us become more like Christ.

Can you trust God's design in your life today?

74

I have learned the secret of being content

BLOOM·WHERE·YOU'RE·PLANTED

I have learned the secret of being content

75

Thank You Father,
for filling my life
to overflowing
with your
love and
joy.

God fills our lives with His love
so we can pour love out on others.
Make a list of the people in your life
who need a good splash of love from you.

The more of God's love and joy we pour out,
the more He pours back in!

This is the day the LORD has made;

welcome

we will rejoice and be glad in it!

PSALM 118:24